101 WAYS
YOU CAN HELP

101 WAYS YOU CAN HELP

How to Offer Comfort and Support
to Those Who Are Grieving

Liz Aleshire

SOURCEBOOKS, INC.
NAPERVILLE, ILLINOIS

In Linda,
And the 100 !
wrap your heap us
y'all. Judy Huse

Bright weaving,
Paula Scardamalia

Published by Sourcebooks, Inc.
P.O. Box 4410, Naperville, Illinois 60567-4410
(630) 961-3900
Fax: (630) 961-2168
www.sourcebooks.com

Library of Congress Cataloging-in-Publication Data

Aleshire, Liz.
  101 ways you can help : how to offer comfort and support to those who are grieving / by Liz Aleshire.
     p. cm.
1. Bereavement. I. Title. II. Title: One hundred one ways you can help. III. Title: One hundred and one ways you can help.
  BF575.G7A52 2009
  155.9'37—dc22

                           2008046209

          Printed and bound in the United States of America.
                 VP 10 9 8 7 6 5 4 3 2 1

To the two most phenomenal bookends any life could deserve: the writing sisters and Nathan Herbert Greenbacker

CONTENTS

FOREWORD

Liz's small apartment was filled with hundreds of hardcover books, most of them nonfiction and all of them read; bright and faded quilts in various stages of completion; and a tabletop Christmas tree, fully decorated. The ornaments were old and looked well loved. Most held pictures of her friends' children and grandchildren.

Keeping the tree up all year didn't stop time. February always brought memories of Nathan's birth. The bookend was August, the month he died. Nathan was Liz's only child. After the horrors of chemotherapy, bone cancer still sliced away his arm and shoulder. Then it took his life. That was 1995. He was sixteen.

As Liz's friends, we always knew she would disappear for several days twice a year. One morning while I was driving us from Connecticut to Massachusetts, she pointed to a nondescript motel and said that's where she spends one weekend every February. Quickly, she explained: they have a heated pool. When we arrived at our destination, I jotted down the name of the motel and tucked it in my purse. Twice a year, Liz teetered on the edge of a dark place. A few times, the quagmire of grief sucked her under. Now I knew at least one hiding place.

Liz was an accountant. Before she became disabled, she worked for a national employment agency that placed her in long-term but temporary assignments. She liked the arrangement. It freed her from any repetitive responsibilities or constraining commitments—as well as from the intimacy that comes with friendships, intimacy that might lead to discussing Nathan and revisiting her terrible loss. The agency liked having her and sent her all over the state. Her experience and her reputation for hard work, not to mention a lightning-speed learning curve on new software, kept her in demand. But she wouldn't work certain days in August. Period.

During those dark days, email gave us a way to stay in touch without being intrusive. Liz wanted and needed her privacy. Her friends needed and wanted to pull her from the quicksand that always threatened to engulf her. We were always vigilant in February and August.

Our antennas were up on Mother's Day, too. Several of us called Liz throughout the weekend, only to reach her answering machine. One of us, Paula, a mother of three grown boys, wrote in her blog that day:

When we give birth to our children, we give birth to hopes and dreams and possibilities. But we also give birth to our worst nightmares and to nights of constant worry. To crossed fingers and endless prayers. And to all the whys and hows and what ifs. Once we give birth, become mothers, we are always mothers. There is never an end. It is who we are for the rest of our lives. Even when those we mother are gone before us. But what do we say to those mothers whose children are gone? "Happy Mother's Day" seems wrong somehow. And yet they remain mothers. Mothers who need to be recognized and honored for the love they gave and for the love they still bear. Mothers who need to be held and supported as they remember the sons and daughters they have lost to illness, violence, and war.

Before Paula posted that entry, she and I shared our concerns about Liz. Something was wrong. We cautioned each other not to overreact, reminding each other that Liz was excited to be writing again and had been making good progress on her manuscript. The manuscript itself was a symbol of how far she had come. She had talked about writing it for several years. I remember asking her why this book was so important when she had other more commercial projects started, including a series of time-travel novels for children. "Because it hurt so bad. People stood and stared at me. I represented every parent's worst nightmare. They couldn't even say a simple, 'I'm sorry.' Their reactions after the funeral were even worse.

Several friends I thought would be supportive couldn't—didn't…" Her thoughts trailed off. I asked how long it took for those friendships to reawaken. "They didn't. I never heard from those women again." A few seconds later she added, with her classic determination, "People don't have to lose friends. And they won't if they just know how to help."

Paula and I noted how freely Liz now talked about Nathan and about his death. She smiled a lot, saying she was finally "in a good place."

We reminded each other of Liz's pattern of sequestering herself to write, and of her commitment to finish the manuscript, expressed just a few weeks earlier on our "Sunday Night Check-In," a weekly email system we created almost two years earlier to keep track of our writing progress.

She reported:

Only wrote three pages on the book and I'm sure that all I did this weekend will have to be severely edited if not completely deleted and done over. By the end of the second page I noticed that it wasn't humorous anymore and it wasn't even light. I'm a little impatient and definitely short tempered. So, I finally figured I'm in an angry phase. The steps in grief are not linear but cyclical. I notice that I continue to rotate through them over the years. I thought it was a blessing that I seemed to miss most of the anger phase. After all, anger isn't much help if it isn't directed somewhere and damned if I could figure out who or what to be angry for/at. I suppose I was naïve to think I could get through this without something rising up. So, I'm taking a few days off to do laundry and then will write, write, write my way through it. It's all part of the journey and, like it or not, I have to work through it so I will. There's a strong feeling of being on the threshold of another large transition. So, I wait, and will continue to just be me…I wish everyone an easier week. But I also hope you have as productive a one as I will.

Liz and I were both writers with full-time day jobs. I appreciated how fiercely she guarded her weekends. So on that Mother's Day in 2008, Paula and I were alert but cautious. In hindsight, I don't think we could have prevented what happened. Still, I think about how things might have been different if I had been at home that weekend instead of in Rhode Island with my daughter and her family. The others in our group live one to three hours from Liz. I live ten minutes away. Liz might have called me on Friday night when the pain started, instead of attributing it to indigestion. She might have called me on Sunday when the pain became excruciating. Instead, she drove herself to the emergency room, where doctors confirmed her fears. She'd had a heart attack. A second attack a week later forever changed her life.

The doctors classified each episode as mild, but when combined with a constitution already compromised by smoking and diabetes, the prognosis was grim: six months to two years.

I notified dozens of Liz's friends, all members of the International Women's Writing Guild (IWWG). Get-well wishes poured in. Among them was a note from Anne. In her big Mother Bear voice, she ordered Liz to get better and finish the manuscript, or she would drive up from New Jersey and finish it for her.

Liz was in the intensive care unit when I delivered Anne's message. With both of us teary eyed, Liz said she'd been thinking about the manuscript. This book was to be her tribute to Nathan. She had outlined the entire book and written most of it. But most wasn't all. Her deadline was May 31.

I called Liz's editor to let her know that Liz was in intensive care, recovering slowly, eager to get back to work on the manuscript. Liz called her editor a few days later, suggested an extension to July 31, and received it.

Because she wasn't allowed near a computer, Liz got creative. She wrote in longhand and on her portable word processor. A number of setbacks followed. In the course of four weeks, she was admitted to three hospitals and a cardiac rehabilitation facility. She had tests upon tests and received multiple opinions. The blockage behind the stent that doctors had inserted ten years earlier was inoperable. Her mother had had a similar condition; she died on the operating table.

Liz and I had what we feared would be our last conversation. She had the same with her sister Nancy Skinnon and with her dear friend Kathy. Nancy is a critical care nurse with a lot of experience in cardiology. Kathy is also a registered nurse and herself a recent breast cancer survivor. The three of us talked about the prognosis. We all knew that no one can say with certainty how much time a person has. We all knew that miracles, though rare, do happen. Would there be one for Liz?

By mid-July, Liz's heart was severely compromised, with only a quarter of it functioning. She had three options. First, go home with meds to manage the pain. Life expectancy would now be only two months. Second, have a ventricular assist device (VAD) installed, one part attached to her heart and the other to a portable device the size and shape of a large fanny pack. With no further plans for surgery, life expectancy was a year, maybe a little longer. Third, have the VAD installed and agree to be considered for a heart transplant. That option carried all sorts of problems, issues, and just plain scary stuff. Plus, with that option, she would then have to wait for someone else to die so she could have a chance to live.

She decided to go home with the meds and wait to die. She and I had a long talk about the implications of that decision, including the fate of *101 Ways You Can Help*. It wasn't that the publication of a book held such importance. This was a special book. Liz had waited since Nathan's death to wrench the memories from her heart and transform them into something that might help others. That night, July 16, I wrote to a small group of our friends, all published authors. We could bring Liz's book to life.

With her permission, I downloaded her files and emailed them to the group. The six of us unanimously agreed that completing this manuscript was a labor of love, not money. We expected nothing. Over the next twenty-four hours, we divided the tasks and got to work. Although Liz wrote with a light, sometimes irreverent, tone, reading her words gave each of us a glimpse into the sorrow she carried since the day her son had died.

We tried to maintain Liz's tone. That said, we are six women with different backgrounds, experiences, perspectives, and spiritual paths. Just as women used to gather around a quilting frame to finish a project begun by one in the group, we stitched our own individual voices into Liz's manuscript.

Nancy, not one of the six scribes, is younger than Liz. Their brother and both parents died years ago, leaving the sisters as the only blood relatives left in that family. They talked about the physical, emotional, and spiritual journeys that awaited. They talked about the childhood brutality that had scarred Liz, and they speculated as to why Nancy had been spared. They had been used as pawns by feuding parents, and the painful memories had separated their hearts for decades. They held hands in reunion. They talked about the future that could be. Optimism wasn't easy for Liz. But just a few days earlier, she had spoken with a former patient whose life blossomed after a heart transplant. When the doctors came for her final decision, Liz looked at Nancy and reached for the brass ring. Maybe, just maybe, she could have a second chance at happiness. She asked to be put on the waiting list for a new heart.

In actuality, being put on a waiting list is no simple matter. Liz would have to pass a battery of tests to ensure that she was healthy enough to receive a new heart. In the meantime, the hospital ordered a VAD and scheduled Liz for surgery on July 29. But on July 25, Liz went into heart failure. The new VAD hadn't arrived. Doctors implanted the only one available, an older contraption with the external portion the size of a small suitcase.

In the weeks that followed, optimism ruled. The doctors said Liz might be able to go home, provided that she had someone with her twenty-four hours a day, seven days a week, for three full weeks. Each companion would first have to take a class on how to operate the VAD should something go awry. Members of the IWWG responded immediately, several of them willing to use vacation time for the cause. In a few days, I had volunteers for a good portion of the three weeks. Those who couldn't help in person donated money to hire a professional aide. A young couple, Mike and Marie Testa, family friends of Liz's, invited her to live with them, offering to convert their dining room into her bedroom. Best of all, their young children adored Liz. All of us, especially Liz, had reason to hope.

But Liz never returned home. She developed an infection in her chest, suffered another heart attack, internal bleeding, and several strokes. In the last few days, it appeared that her leg would have to be amputated.

For much of that time, members of IWWG kept Hartford Hospital's CareGram service busy with email messages, and some drove hundreds of miles to visit. Paula called from New York almost every day, first to give Liz a chance to vent her anger and sadness, and second to read another chapter in a novel by one of Liz's favorite suspense authors, Clive Cussler. The reading always calmed and relaxed her enough to let her sleep. Anne drove up from New Jersey with her sense of humor and warm support. Marsha drove down from Boston with a laptop so Liz could connect with the world via email now that she was allowed to use a computer. Unfortunately, Liz didn't have the strength to hold a cup of water, much less operate a keyboard. Kathy came to the hospital almost every other day, once in a while with the chocolate milkshake Liz craved. I printed a copy of the book cover so Liz would have a visual reminder that the book of her heart would soon be a reality.

Despite her love of M&M's, Liz did not believe in sugar-coating anything. We spoke candidly about death. Ironically, before she got sick, she often talked about creating a website called Living Eulogies, a place where a person could post a loving tribute to someone while that someone was still alive and could enjoy reading it.

A few hours before she died, Paula, our friend Carol Chaput, my daughter Laurie Neronha, and I gathered around Liz's bedside. She was unconscious. I was certain that on some level she could hear us. So, one at a time, we told her how she had influenced our lives. We said we were happy that she and Nathan would be reunited. We sang to her. We told her we loved her.

Laurie was the last to leave the room. "Mom," she called out, "Liz is crying!" The nurse rushed in, surveyed the situation, and told us we were mistaken. The fluid was merely a physical reaction. I don't doubt the medical explanation. Nor do I doubt that Liz heard us and that her tears were to say good-bye.

Liz died at 12:12 a.m. on Monday, October 13, 2008. She was fifty-nine years old.

Three weeks before her death, Liz asked me to conduct her funeral, if the need arose. After she died, I, in turn, called on the other five writers. Marsha created a memorial website for those who could not attend, as well as a memorial video to play at the service. Judy flew in from Wisconsin to share with others in attendance at the funeral the experience of the day that she and Liz discovered they were both members of the sorority no one wants to join—that of mothers whose sons had died. Each of us spoke about Liz in terms of a favorite quilt pattern. Though most of the service was joyful, we still needed to shore up each other and Nancy. We needed Liz's book.

So here it is. Don't worry. "Finish your friend's manuscript" is not one of the helpful tips Liz included in this book.

Adding those final "stitches" is, however, the task the six of us treasured.

—Zita Christian

—The friends: Kathy Barach, Marsha Browne, Zita Christian, Judy Huge, Paula Chaffee Scardamalia, Anne Frazier Walradt

ACKNOWLEDGMENTS

It would be impossible for me to have this book enter the world without acknowledging six of the strongest, most loyal, professional, and dedicated women in the world—my writing sisters: Kathy Barach, Marsha Browne, Zita Christian, Judy Huge, Paula Chaffee Scardamalia, and Anne Frazier Walradt.

It would be an intolerable omission for me not to thank the other half of this important publishing process. For her willingness to adapt, senior editor Shana Drehs and everyone else at Sourcebooks, Inc., who was involved in the project.

Thanks to the members of the Sunday Night Check-In (SNCI) group: Judy Adourian, Zita Christian, Chris Peter, and Paula Chaffee Scardamalia. Thanks also to John C. Carmon, past president and current director of the National Funeral Directors Association; Michael A. Goncalves, vice-president and senior financial consultant for Webster Bank Investments; Sue Gebo, MPH, RD, a consulting nutritionist; Laurie Neronha, herbalist and aesthetician; Linda Kelly, program director at the Center for Grieving Children in Portland, Maine; Mary Keane, former executive director and founder of Mary's Place in Windsor, Connecticut; Robert W. Gillikin, CLU, financial adviser; Glenda Baker, author and editor; Darrelyn Gunzburg, author of *Life after Grief*; Carolyn Casey, author of *Making the Gods Work for You*; and Carol Chaput, Buddhist and artist.

For thirty years of the best teaching, mentoring, and support, I am proud to acknowledge the International Women's Writing Guild for leading me on this path.

And finally, to my own sister Nancy Skinnon, who took over the responsibility of my care in the hospital, all my personal business, and in a way, smoothed the road, making it easier for the writing sisters to play their part in getting this book finished.

INTRODUCTION

So Why Should You Listen to Me?

I needed this book. I really, *really* needed this book about fifteen years ago when my only child Nathan died of cancer at age sixteen. But it wasn't out there. I read a ton of books about grief and bereavement and what I should do to help myself. But there was nothing I could give friends, family members, organizations I belonged to, the people I worked with, or the members at my church on how they could help me. It was painfully evident, except for a couple of courageous, persistent friends, that no one knew how to help me.

See, we don't talk about death. No one's interested in talking about death. Most of all me! According to D. Brookes Cowan, a senior lecturer in sociology at the University of Vermont, end-of-life care specialist, and part of the team that produced the critically acclaimed 2004 documentary *Pioneers of Hospice: Changing the Face of Dying*, death has replaced sex as the number-one taboo topic of conversation in America.

That is in direct contradiction to the idea that the more

people we share our sorrow with—the number quoted is usually one hundred—the more healing occurs. In the past fifteen years, I've told maybe twenty people the agonizing story of my son's death. I've got eighty to go. The problem is finding those additional eighty people willing to listen and talk about death in general and my bereavement in particular.

If we don't talk about it, how will we ever learn how to be one of the one hundred who help others when death occurs? Because I knew my loss wasn't the first death people had encountered, I was confused as to why they didn't know how to help me even though they wanted to.

Over the past fifteen years, we've suffered through numerous school shootings, mass murders, mine collapses, devastating losses from tsunamis, and war. After September 11, 2001, I was sure someone would see the need for this book and that quickly we'd have the definitive work on how anyone could help the bereaved. I waited in vain. The book never came out.

As a writer, the answer became clear. I'd have to write it myself. I was reluctant. While I, unfortunately, could speak with the voice of authority (after all, I've lived it—been there, done that, burned the T-shirt), I struggled with *how* to write it. As my writer friends told me I should write a book about my experience, all I thought was, *Who the hell would read a depressing book like that?*

Well, I'm described as having quite the sense of humor. So I outlined and pitched the book as written in a light, humorous, and sometimes irreverent tone. A humorous book about death? Could I do that? Any doubts I had about my ability to write this book with that voice vanished as soon as I typed in Tip #1, the first way to help the bereaved. It was a challenge, but it was fun and relatively easy after that. I had, after all, been writing this book in my head for fifteen years!

While this book is 90 percent things people should do to help the bereaved (the *do*s), there are some things that should be strictly avoided (the *don't*s.) They've happened to me, and they've happened to every bereaved person I've met. I managed to keep the *don't*s light, too, I hasten to add, but all of these *don't*s are real.

Yep, I really needed this book. Now I have it. And so do you. It's a reference work you can keep on the shelf for years, to help you and the people close to you weather whatever life or, rather, death, throws at you. It even includes an appendix that provides the manner of dress, particular customs, and a kind of code of conduct at funerals for nine different religious groups and nonreligious ones as well, from the Baha'i to the Unitarian Universalist. So if you are on your way out the door now to go to a viewing or funeral and want to know if you are dressed correctly, then go ahead and flip immediately to the appendix. Otherwise, here is how to read this book.

Chapter 1 lists eleven things everyone should know and do to help the bereaved. Read that.

Chapter 2 lists eleven things everyone should absolutely *not* say to the bereaved. I call them the Atrocious Eleven. Read that chapter—especially if you are on your way out the door to a viewing or funeral. Please.

Chapter 3 has ten tips for someone you know just a little, like someone who belongs to your garden club or the gym where you work out. So that chapter is useful for everyone. Read it.

Chapter 4 has thirteen tips to help you support the bereaved who is your co-worker or employee.

Chapter 5 has twenty-one tips for if the bereaved is your neighbor, and chapter 6 has thirty-five tips for if the bereaved is your best friend or family member.

Do you see a pattern here? Yes, the closer you are to the bereaved, the more you can do for him or her. Isn't that nice to know? And, in fact, many of the tips for the bereaved who isn't as close to you are also useful for the bereaved who is your best friend.

So here's the thing. I divided these tips into chapters so you can refer quickly to the section most appropriate and helpful for you, depending on the degree of intimacy of your relationship to the bereaved or the deceased. So go ahead and flip to that chapter if you need that information right now. But the bottom line? *Read the whole book.* Because sooner or later, the bereaved will be a golf buddy, and a co-worker, and a neighbor, and a best friend.

Please use it. Please encourage others to use it. I need eighty more listeners. And someday, you'll need your one hundred. Let's train them now.

Some Things to Keep in Mind While Reading This Book

Journalists, and I do think of myself as a journalist, are foremost charged with the responsibility of objectivity. We're not supposed to take sides. We're supposed to offer up the facts and nothing but the facts so the reader can make up his or her mind on the basis of the facts. That said, I've found some biases running rampant in my book and want to point them out to you.

First, it will be obvious that I value quality of life as exponentially more important than quantity of life. If you disagree, wonderful! It's a discussion that needs to take place more often and more in depth than it has been. When you come across my bias, take it with a grain of salt. We can agree to disagree on this one, OK?

Second, try as I might, there is an underlying bias toward Protestantism in this book. That's how I was raised, and while I watched for it and tried to eliminate it, some of the basic *do*s in the book arise from a definite Protestant experience—hence the appendix at the end of the book listing the differences in other cultures in funeral rites and ceremonies. I think I redeem myself there.

Third, those pronouns! While trying to be all inclusive, I ran smack into the *he*, *she*, *they*, *them*, and *their* pronoun controversy. I really hate the *he or she* thing. Because I'm a woman, I found I naturally gravitated toward the feminine pronoun *she*. *This won't do*, I admonished myself. I tried to make sure there was an equal use of *he* and *she* throughout; I hope no one is offended.

Fourth, I made a conscious decision not to use a nationally known expert when I needed one. Almost every expert quoted in the book works or lives within twenty miles of my hometown. My purpose was to prove that you, the reader, can find creditable, knowledgeable, and experienced doctors, psychologists, grief counselors, and caregivers in your backyard as I did in mine. What good are nationally known experts when they are not readily available to you? I didn't have time to wait for Dr. Phil to become interested in my situation. I needed help immediately. Working with your local pool of experts ensures you can get help when you need it.

That's it, reader. Make up your own mind as you go.

1

THE BASIC DOS

The next three paragraphs are all you'll read in this book about actual death and grief. Promise!

The following statement is perhaps the only one ever made that elicits 100 percent agreement across all fifty states in our nation:

Death sucks!

You think so. I think so. Everyone thinks so. Everyone wants to avoid the rituals of dying: the wake, the funeral, and, all too often, the bereaved, as though death is contagious. It's not. You can't catch death cooties or depression by participating in the rites and ceremonies that help the bereaved. Oh, you thought the wake and funeral were only for the deceased? Wrong! Funeral ceremonies pay homage to the deceased, but you're really going because the presence of friends and loved ones are a true comfort to those grieving the loss. Think of attendance at these ceremonies as not for the dead person but for those left living. Life is about helping others and being helped in return when you need it. There isn't anything you can do for the unfortunate person lying in the casket. But you can help the family and friends standing next to it.

Which brings us to grief. It also sucks! If you're not the bereaved, it's easy to dismiss funeral rites as morbid, depressing, even barbaric. We want desperately to avoid them because of the feelings of discomfort and mortality they raise in us. For the bereaved these rites are a source of great comfort. For a few days following the death of a loved one, the bereaved is not alone. "A grief shared is a sorrow halved" has become a cliché because it's so damn true! The wake and funeral are an opportunity for the bereaved to get hugs, to hear anecdotes, and to be awed and comforted by the number of people who care about her or about her loved one. If you've lost a loved one, you know exactly what I mean. If you haven't yet experienced bereavement, trust me! Your presence is a priceless source of comfort, and this book tells you what to do, how to do it, and when to do it, so you don't end up putting your foot in your mouth or causing more pain for those who are grieving.

This chapter covers the universal basics of helping the bereaved no matter what his relationship is to you.

1.
Accept that you can't fix it, and stop trying

Oh, how we wish we could take away the pain of grief! But unless you have a few miracles in your pocket and can raise the dead or remove the pain of loss, you'd better accept the fact that you can't fix the problem of death. It's precisely when people think they can fix the problem that they say or do things that cause more pain for the bereaved (see chapter 2, on *don'ts*). The bereaved don't hold it against you: the bereaved know you desperately want to help them and that you're operating from a heart full of compassion. Even if you can't accept your inability to fix it, fake it. Adopt an attitude of helpless compassion—not one of *here comes the hero*.

2.
Go to the viewing or wake

The wake is an opportunity for friends, co-workers, neighbors, and relatives to express condolences to the bereaved. For most religions, a wake usually takes place in a funeral home (the appendix covers the rites of other cultures and religions that have different customs). Sometimes the wake is split into two sessions, such as from three to five in the afternoon and then again from seven to nine in the evening. This allows people who work during the day the opportunity to attend the wake in the evening. Increasingly, though, people are opting for one four-hour calling period, say, from three in the afternoon to seven at night, which can accommodate everyone's schedules at once.

A newspaper obituary may have funeral information, but

don't rely on it for directions to the funeral home. If you aren't familiar with the funeral home, or if it's in another city, you can either call the home and ask for directions or use the Internet to find your way. And it helps if you can accompany someone else you know who knew the bereaved or the deceased. The cliché that there's safety in numbers is also true. You'll feel less awkward with someone else along.

The first thing you'll encounter when you enter the funeral home is the guest register. Please, please, please sign your name. The bereaved are in a state of shock. Unless you sign the guest book they may be hard pressed to remember that you attended. Months and even years later, the bereaved can revisit the comfort they received at the wake by reading the guest book and seeing your name.

You'll smell the flowers first. If the deceased or bereaved was famous or popular in the community or had many friends or an extended family, there may be so many flowers that the smell, however wonderful individually, is collectively overwhelming. Be prepared for this. It's no reason to turn tail and run!

There will be a large room filled with conversation groupings of easy chairs and couches or just rows of folding chairs. At the far end of the room, usually, is the casket. The flowers surround the casket, and the family sits or stands nearby in a receiving line of sorts. If there's no one in line, immediately walk up to the family. If there is a line, maybe a long one, you don't have to stand in it, increasing your own discomfort tenfold for every minute you wait. Choose one of those chairs in the middle of the room, and sit for awhile. This gives the added benefit of watching the people who arrived before you to see what they do.

Be prepared for an open casket and seeing the deceased's body. I find an open casket more than slightly creepy and insisted on a closed casket for my son. Remember that you don't have to go up to the open casket (or the closed one either for that matter!) if it's just too hard for you. It's also appropriate to stand or kneel by the casket and pray, meditate, or remember the times you shared with the deceased, but it isn't required. No one will think less of you if you don't go up to the casket. Give your condolences to the bereaved, and go right back to one of the seats. It's comforting to the bereaved to see people sitting. An empty calling room is painful. If you've noticed that not too many people have stayed after visiting with the bereaved, be a good soul and sit for a while to up the numbers in the room.

Often there is a small table near the casket that has a pile of cards on it. The wake is a good place to leave a sympathy card. It saves having to mail it, and the card can be read at the leisure of the bereaved, reminding them of your presence at the wake and of your care and support when they most needed it.

If you meet someone you know at the wake and he or she is also sitting, join that person. Feel free to talk, catch up, or exchange stories about your relationship to the deceased or the bereaved. It's also OK to laugh. The bereaved need to laugh.

It's a healing thing. Hearing the buzz of talk and some laughter reminds them that their friends and family are with them.

At some point, it'll be time for you to leave. Some people go back up and say good-bye to the bereaved with another condolence. This isn't required. If you've said everything appropriate to the bereaved, you can go ahead and leave.

To be absolutely sure that you do the right thing at a wake, either check out the appendix of this book or call the funeral home. John C. Carmon, the past president and current director of the National Funeral Directors Association, says a call to the funeral home for this purpose is appropriate.

"The funeral home personnel should know what differences there are from the average wake," he told me. "They'll be very accommodating to such a call and explain just what the person has to do." Don't assume that every religion does a wake the same way. There can be huge differences in customs. Check them out beforehand instead of blindly attending and perhaps committing some horrendous faux pas and creating more pain for the bereaved.

3.
Just say, "I'm sorry for your loss"

Remember Tip #1: Accept that you can't fix it, and stop trying. It's during the condolence-giving portion of the wake that hero-on-the-way syndrome can prompt a friend to say something hurtful. Although the vast majority of funerals are held because of the deceased's or bereaved's religion, it's best to stay away from any pronouncements of religion. Even the most faithful are prone to at least a mild crisis of faith at the time of a death. So leave unspoken such statements as "He's in a better place," "God must have needed her for something," "Sometimes the answer to prayer is no," "Maybe God did this so we'd learn something," and "God never gives us more than we can handle." Speaking from personal experience, I found those statements—and I've heard them all many times—very painful. I don't believe in a supreme being who micromanages by picking a child to die for some purpose known only to that being, and it's possible the bereaved you know feel something similar. I've talked with many bereaved, and they have also heard such statements and felt the same pain.

Also, there are some nonspiritual statements that society has told us should help the bereaved, but they don't. Avoid comparison (one-upmanship) statements such as, "I worked with someone who lost her brother, mother, and father all within a month!" The fact that someone else is worse off doesn't make the bereaved feel better. But it could make them feel guilty for grieving "too much." Guilt over grieving too much is something that forces the bereaved into Academy Award–winning performances of being over it, as does hearing statements about "getting right back to work," "putting all this behind you and moving on," or the worst: "You're young; you can have more children (find another husband, make a new best friend)."

Grieving takes more time than the days starting with the death and ending with the burial. It can take years. And children, spouses, and friends are not interchangeable, as though the bereaved could go to the store and buy another square peg that will exactly fill the square hole left behind in the bereaved's heart.

Remember, you can't fix it, so don't try. The best thing to say is a simple "I'm sorry for your loss." Believe me when I say that the people ahead of you in line have already said one of the previous no-no's. Your "I'm sorry," coupled with a firm handshake, a touch to the arm, or a hug, will be a welcome relief.

4.

Tell an anecdote

Stop thinking about how much you don't want to go, and start thinking of an anecdote you can share with the bereaved about the deceased. In the Jewish religion, mourners spend up to a week sitting shivah, a process in which the bereaved stay at home and the consolers visit to share stories, anecdotes, and even tall tales about the deceased. Whether or not the bereaved is Jewish, the folks left behind love to hear stories about their loved one. If you knew only the deceased and not the bereaved, introduce yourself, and then tell him something your friend did: "I'll never forget the time that Donna used her niblick to..." "George was the best quilter in our group. I remember he worked a year on that purple and orange quilt only to…" or "The last time we bowled, the other team was beating us. So Mary took an elastic band and a cashew and…" (Of course, if your memory isn't flattering to the deceased, it might be better to stick to the "I'm sorry" as discussed earlier.)

If you didn't know the deceased but know the bereaved, repeat something to them that they shared with you in the past about their loved one: "I'll never forget the story you told me about how Bob took that can of Spam and…" "You know, I still laugh about the time Sherry quilted her wall hanging to her skirt, and when she stood up…" "I remember how happy you were when Stan sent you flowers at work, but you called him up to complain about…"

It's perfectly all right, in fact it's a good thing, to make the bereaved laugh. Laughter, like crying, is a healing act. It releases pent-up emotions that can cause permanent damage to the bereaved if they don't have a way to release them.

5.
Let her cry

Again speaking from experience, it's a real stab in the heart to have someone tell you: "Now, now, don't cry!" The bereaved know, all too painfully well, that people get very uncomfortable when someone cries. We know that truth so well that we'll pretend we're not on the verge of tears just to make you feel comfortable! But if I, as the bereaved, can't cry at the wake, when there are people who care about me around to rub my back, hold my hand, and give me a hug, when can I cry? Normally the only time the bereaved feel it's polite to cry is when they're alone, which just makes the sadness and pain stronger and harder to bear. So buck up, folks! Let the bereaved cry. Cry with her if that's your reaction to people in tears. Depending on your relationship with the bereaved, hold her hand, put an arm around her shoulder, and let her cry on yours. Give her a hug while she cries. Until someone does it for you (may that be a long time from now), you can't know what a comfort it is to have someone just stay with you while you cry. Again, you don't have to say anything, just let her cry. Strongly curb the urge to use any of the platitudes discussed earlier! If you absolutely must open your mouth, then just say, "I'm so sorry for your loss."

6.
Go ahead and give him a hug!

Hugs are almost always appropriate at a wake. If a hug is just too intimate for your relationship with the bereaved, when you shake hands, use both of yours. Or simply touch the bereaved's arm. Physical contact from friends and family is another opportunity for the bereaved to heal. The simplest touch says that you care, so don't avoid appropriately touching the bereaved, even briefly. I have more to say about the value of hugs in Tip #77.

7.
Dress appropriately

And I don't mean all in black. These days black isn't worn to funerals as much as it was in the past. (I wore a red dress to both my son's wake and funeral because he always complained that I wore too much black.)

In every movie or television show I've watched that includes a wake or funeral scene, there's always a gorgeous female attending in a miniskirt and skimpy halter top. Or there is a handsome, studly male in a shirt and sport jacket, but the shirt is unbuttoned to almost the navel to display a well-muscled chest and just the right amount of supposedly sexy chest hair. But this is reality. Avoid the temptation to follow the Hollywood-suggested wake and funeral attire (check out the appendix in the back instead).

Ladies, show less: less leg, less midriff, less cleavage. Slacks are appropriate; a dress or suit is nice but isn't required.

Gentlemen, button up. Dressing appropriately doesn't require a three-piece suit. An unwrinkled shirt or sweater with crisp chinos is fine. A sports jacket, if you have one, is a plus but not required.

Children, especially teens, are a different matter. Neat and clean is still the order of the day, but if your children are willing to go to a wake or funeral, this isn't the time to start World War III over the way they're dressed. Make sure all the important parts are covered and nothing is unduly ripped, frayed, or stained. If suits and dresses aren't required for the adults, then they aren't required for the kids either. The current dress fad or fashion, as long as it's neat and clean, may raise the confidence level of children and make it possible for them to attend the funeral rites. Be proud of them for their willingness to go and pay their respects.

Someone inappropriately dressed diverts attention away from the bereaved. Remember, you're attending to help the loved ones left behind, not to make a fashion statement for yourself.

8.
Go to the funeral

Yes, I said go to the funeral. I know you already sucked it up and went to the wake when you really didn't want to. And I know you don't want to go to a funeral. Well, here's a secret from me to you. I don't want to go to funerals either. Neither does anyone else. So there's comfort in numbers, right? At least you'll know you're among people of a like mind.

Some funerals start at the funeral home. In fact, for some, the entire funeral service is conducted at the funeral home. Some will start at a church. You have the option of talking with the bereaved again or just sitting down. Follow the service as best you can. You don't have to be a Catholic to attend a funeral mass or a Buddhist to attend their funeral rites. Often there's an order of worship, a bulletin, or funeral service papers stacked at the door that will be explicit about what to do and when. Do only what you feel comfortable doing. You can tastefully avoid any part of the service you don't feel you can participate in by simply staying in your seat until that section is completed.

Wherever the funeral is held, the funeral home staff may approach you and ask whether you're driving to the graveside service, if there is one. Please attend. I hear you: "What! Something else I don't want to do?" Yes, I'm strongly recommending that you do one more thing to help the bereaved. Your presence at the graveside ceremony is greatly appreciated by the bereaved, as this is the last moment he'll be in the physical presence of his loved one's body.

The funeral home staff may take your name and/or license plate number. After the service (there's more on services in the appendix), they may call your name and give you instructions on where to line up your car with the other attendees. If not, simply wait your turn to get your car in line behind others and follow them out into the street. You'll be sitting in your car for a few minutes because the last to leave the funeral home or church are the bereaved and the casket, and they lead the procession. The funeral procession will lead you to the cemetery depending on arrangements the family made.

At the cemetery, watch the rest of the attendees or wait for the funeral home staff to tell you to get out of your car and walk to the graveside. This part of the ceremonies is usually very short. If the family has made arrangements for a gathering at their home or a restaurant after the graveside ceremony, it'll be announced now. If you feel up to it, say one more "I'm sorry" to the bereaved. Then you can get in your car and head for the bereaved's home or the restaurant.

"There's more?" you ask. Hey, in for a penny, in for a pound, right? Don't worry, very soon you'll be able to go home or back to work. I promise. The gathering at the home or restaurant after a funeral is simply another way to keep people around the bereaved on what is likely the worst day of their lives. Mingle, talk some more, tell some more stories, eat something, and then say your good-byes.

I guarantee that, if you're open to it, the experience will give you a warm glow of a good deed well done. You didn't try to fix it, you didn't say or do anything embarrassing, and you helped a friend through a difficult day. Pat yourself on the back.

9.
When it's OK to bring children

I'm of the "it's never too soon" school when it comes to exposing children to wakes and funerals. They are a good opportunity to talk with children about death and whatever religious beliefs you hold on the subject. I was six when my grandfather died. I wasn't allowed to go to the funeral, and there was no discussion about death. My grandfather was just gone. I learned later that my mother kept us from the funeral to protect us, but I was crushed when I couldn't go with her to the funeral home. Somehow it made his loss even more bewildering.

It's perfectly OK to bring children to the wake or funeral if they knew either the deceased or the bereaved—and if their behavior will match the solemnity of the occasion. Keep children close to you at all times. Explain ahead of time what to expect. By all means, take children up to the bereaved so that they can offer the "I'm sorry for your loss" condolence. Children are a blessing at funeral rites. They remind us that life goes on.

10.
When it's not OK to bring children

Funerals are not a spectator sport or a classroom. If your children didn't know the deceased or bereaved but attend the wake or funeral anyway, it'll be obvious you're using someone else's bad day as a practice session. And it will be meaningless to your child.

Also, it's not OK to bring squirmy, hyperactive, uncontrollable children. Be sure children are old enough to understand basic manners, and don't allow them to run around the room or do cartwheels past the casket. If your children are well behaved when you go out to dinner, then they have suitable manners to attend the wake or funeral of someone they knew.

What if you want to go to the funeral but can't find a babysitter? Well, you have a couple of options. One option, of course, is to not go. If you choose that option, then consider calling the bereaved a day ahead of time to offer your condolences along with your apologies and reason for not attending the funeral.

Another option is to find out whether the church or funeral home offers a babysitting service for such occasions. Sometimes a church member who doesn't know the deceased will volunteer to care for children. Or you can check to see whether other parents you know will be attending and ask whether you can share a sitter and the cost. Finally, if all else fails, volunteer to be the babysitter for your children and others' at the funeral service. This way you support the bereaved and are still part of the community ritual.

11.
When you can't go to the funeral

Hey, it happens. Maybe you were out of town, sick, giving a huge presentation to a new important client, or your child graduated that day. In any event, you couldn't make it to any of the ceremonies immediately following the death. What to do?

Sending a sympathy card with a simple handwritten note with "So sorry for your loss" above your signature is an excellent way to show you care. Some sympathy cards go over the top with sentiment—avoid sappy cards in favor of a short statement of sympathy.

Sending flowers to the funeral home or church is always appropriate when circumstances dictate that you can't make it to the ceremonies. Pay attention, though, to family requests for something other than flowers, like making a donation to a suggested charity. It doesn't help the bereaved to have to deal with flower arrangements they don't want. You can check with your local horticulture society for recommendations on reputable, reliable florists and for suggestions on types of flowers. If you'd also like to send a garden plant to the house, that's a good idea, too, and the society can make suggestions about appropriate and easy-to-care-for plants.

Perhaps a fruit basket would be even better. The bereaved, in a state of shock, won't be up for eating much, but fruit is a nice, light, easily digestible, sweet food they usually can stomach.

Often these days obituaries will direct you to the deceased's favorite charity. As suggested earlier, you might want to make a donation in lieu of flowers. Make sure when you send your check that you tell the charity who the donation is in memory of and give the address of the bereaved so that they receive a notice of the donation. No charity tells the bereaved how much you gave, just that you gave.

And if none of these ideas feels right to you, consider giving the gift of a service, such as several visits from a housecleaning service, or a week from a personal meal service, or even a month of movies. You may want to get together with others to make your budget for such services stretch further.

Any of these options let the bereaved know you are thinking of them, even when you can't attend the service, but whatever you do, don't spend more than you can afford.

Well, those are the basics. You're now amply prepared to do several very nice things for the bereaved and honor the memory of the deceased. But, as you'll see in the remainder of this book, grief and the state of shock that comes with it don't end with the funeral. The bereaved might mourn for weeks, months, or years. In truth, the pain of loss never goes away. It isn't something you survive or overcome. You don't recover from it. Over time you just get more used to the pain and can go on to live your new life. In the early days though, the bereaved need us more than ever.

Read on! There's more that you can do and none of it is as hard as the wake or funeral.

2

THE BASIC DON'TS

Like clichés and old wives' tales, the *don't*s in the eleven tips in this chapter contain a grain of truth. But that grain of truth is salt in the wounds of the brokenhearted. Society has trained us to use these statements to comfort the grieving. But just like clichés and old wives' tales, the Atrocious Eleven should be ignored. Some of them will surprise you. They are so tightly woven into the fabric of our society that it seems sacrilegious to denounce them.

Hmm. Let's see if I can find a polite way to say this...Nope, there is no polite or original way to explain how much these statements hurt. In the words of an old cliché—they are like kicking the bereaved when they are already down. We continue using these statements because the people we say them to offer us a measure of grace we just don't deserve. The bereaved know that we say these things to them because we really believe they'll help. The bereaved know we are speaking from full hearts. Even though they're sorely tempted to punch us in the nose, they smile, thank us, and wish there was a book they could give us to set us straight.

For each of the Atrocious Eleven you could say to the bereaved, I'll tell you what the bereaved are feeling when they hear them and why.

12.
Don't say, "She's in a better place"

Ah, the guilt trip. What the bereaved will never say out loud: "I don't care if she's in Tahiti belting back margaritas and surrounded by handsome hunks. I want her here."

Oh, yeah, you meant heaven, Valhalla, Elysium, paradise, Summerland, or Happy Hunting Grounds, didn't you? How can the bereaved disagree, especially as this is usually said at the wake or funeral (as are all of the Atrocious Eleven)? We all know life is tough. So far, though, it's still preferable to death. In a state of shocked selfishness, the bereaved simply wants his loved one back. Having her back would ease his pain, and at the moment, that's all that matters. The atrocious "she's in a better place" forces the bereaved to somehow feel happy that his loved one has left his arms, left him behind, and gone on to some wild and wonderful party—without him! Why should he be happy about that? It's nothing more than a guilt trip for those who are grieving.

13.
Don't say, "At least he went quickly"

What the bereaved will never say out loud: "Yeah, so quickly I never got to say 'I love you' just one more time!"

The person who is grieving suffers whether the Grim Reaper lingered or showed up suddenly. I've experienced both. A heart attack took my brother. His sudden death left me with the grief of not having time to say good-bye. At the time, I thought that was the worst way to lose a loved one. Then my son got cancer. The disease took him slowly. We all saw death coming, but that didn't make it any easier to bear. And that leads us to the next atrocious statement.

14.
Don't say, "At least her suffering is over"

What the bereaved will never say out loud: "Well, she could have suffered a little longer!"

This is another kind of guilt trip. No one wants a loved one to suffer. Let me repeat that: no one wants a loved one to suffer. But again, if we had our druthers, and if we were honest, we'd admit to preferring perhaps a little more suffering instead of the permanent separation of death. See, there's that in-shock selfishness issue again. When we learned my son's cancer had spread to his lungs and he was terminal, doctors told us he could live a year longer if he continued the treatments that made his life a living hell. If I made the decision that was best for me, I'd have kept on with the treatments. After all, and this may sound callous, but here goes: I wouldn't be the one suffering. I'd still have my son. If I made the decision that was best for him, I'd have him with me only a few more weeks. He died in two. I still have moments when I wish I had been selfish.

So, down with guilt trips!

15.

Don't say, "What doesn't kill us makes us stronger"

What the bereaved won't say out loud: "You forget the walking dead!"

This one might pass muster after ten years or so of adapting to a new life without the loved one, but it sure doesn't work in the early days of grief. Moving through grief to living with hope again takes many, many baby steps. Adapting to a new, lonely life feels impossible. It's such a slow—agonizingly slow—process that the bereaved can't recognize when he's made progress. He's pretty sure that the light at the end of the tunnel is the headlight of an oncoming train. The bereaved, no matter how he appears, does not feel strong. He doesn't feel brave. He doesn't feel alive. He doesn't feel like a survivor, like he's recovered, or like he's healed. He doesn't even feel better. This statement implies that strength is the prize the bereaved should keep his eye on. Too often the price of strength in the face of tragedy means losing the ability to ever feel joy. This atrocious statement trivializes the pain the bereaved feels and reduces his journey through grief to a few quick trips to a health club.

So, let 'em be weak, and let 'em lean on you.

16.
Don't say, "I knew someone who…"

What usually follows this statement is some horrendous story about multiple family deaths from tragic circumstances, probably a mass murder. What the bereaved won't say out loud: "Someone's worse off than me? By golly, now I feel better!"

Grow up! It's a rare person who can comfort him- or herself with the thought that someone has a worse life. Let's face it—most of us aren't that nice! Our pain is our pain, and because it's ours, it's the worst pain in the world. The bereaved, wrapped in her gloom, frankly doesn't and won't believe that anyone is suffering more than she is. And guess what—she'd be right! Forcing her to acknowledge that there are people worse off than she is at this moment in her life trivializes what she's feeling. When we use this statement, we're really saying: "Buck up, kiddo! You haven't got it so bad after all!" Well, buck up, kiddo, and knock this one permanently off the "supposed to be comforting" list.

17.

Don't say, "He must have died to teach us something"

What the bereaved won't say out loud: "Yeah—that death sucks!"

I have a hard time with the theory that God, Buddha, Allah, Mother Nature, or whatever other supreme being the world might embrace, micromanages our lives to the point that He/She/It/They will randomly pick my loved one to die to teach somebody else a lesson. Nope, that one doesn't fly with me. I'm constantly amazed at the people who say, "I never knew how much my mother (or father, brother, sister, husband) meant to me until she died." Why not? What's wrong with us? Why don't we recognize the importance of family and friends until after they're gone? It wasn't a lesson I needed to learn, and I resented it when people thought that saying so would help me.

So, even though you might have learned something from death, don't burden the bereaved with the thought that his loved one died to teach him something. Remember it, act on it, live by what you've learned, but don't expect the bereaved to find comfort in such a statement.

18.
Don't say, "He (or She, It, or They) must have needed her"

What the bereaved won't say out loud: "For what? And why didn't He (or She, It, or They) just do whatever needed doing?

See, a core belief of many religions is that the supreme being is omniscient and omnipotent. So why would any supreme being need my mere-mortal loved one, with hair growing out of his nose, who couldn't cook worth a damn, and was helpless at math? Or the wife who got out of breath just looking at a flight of stairs? Or the father who needed someone to mow the lawn for him? The grandmother who couldn't even turn a computer on? The brother whom dogs hated? The friend who couldn't say "thank you" if someone handed her a prompt card? Why in heaven would someone in heaven need our imperfect, flawed loved ones?

Like the ones before, this statement attributes the micro-management of everyone's lives to whatever supreme being *you* believe in. There's no guarantee that the bereaved has the same belief. It also makes the bereaved feel guilty for even thinking she needed her loved one more than God did.

19.

Don't say, "You should be happy for how long you did have him"

What the bereaved won't say out loud: "I am. I just wanted him longer."

Good grief! There is no right age to die. Whether the deceased lived a hundred days or a hundred years, we, the loved ones left behind, still prefer them alive. In chapter 6, you'll read about something called "complicated grief," which affects those who suffer a sudden, untimely, or violent loss. I'm not discounting that at all. What I am saying is that there's never enough time to be with loved ones. We can't ever get enough of them. Sure, we call some deaths timely, especially those that come with old age and a life well lived. Depending on the spiritual views of the bereaved, she may be able to celebrate the life of the loved one while also mourning that person's death. But don't say that it was time. There would always be something to learn, something to laugh at, something to live. There's never enough time to be with a loved one.

20.

Don't say, "C'mon, pal, men don't cry"

What the bereaved won't say out loud: "They don't heal, either. What a waste!"

Telling the bereaved, man or woman, not to cry robs him or her of one of the outlets that has the most power to heal. In my opinion and experience, only listening to the bereaved talk about his loved one surpasses crying as the perfect release valve for his grief. I don't know a safer way to deflate anger, pain, frustration, helplessness, or grief than through tears. And because we use this statement only for our own comfort, not to comfort the bereaved, it's doubly ridiculous. I hear you; you can't stand to see someone cry. It makes you tear up, too. And there's something wrong with that?

To quote Sally Field: "Buckle up; this is a story coming." I went to a grief support group for four meetings. A priest facilitated the hospital-based group. There were about six other people who attended besides me. I introduced myself and explained why I was there. The other folks introduced themselves and filled me in on their paths through grief.

I wasn't too trusting. I had heard, "Please, don't cry," so many times by then that I was determined not to cry anywhere. After the third meeting, though, I felt comfortable enough to let it all out.

The evening of that meeting a new couple attended. It didn't stop me. If you can't cry at a grief support group, where can you cry? I told my worst fears, and yes, I cried. The other members were supportive. They said all the right things. As the meeting ended, the facilitator turned to the new members and said, "Our meetings aren't usually this emotional. I hope we haven't scared you off with our tears and that you'll come back next week." Huh? I'd been the only one who had broken down. I was the one who finished the one box of Kleenex on the table. I was the only one who had cried. There was no "us" being emotional. There were no "our" tears. Just me. I looked around at the other members, who just sat there. *Well*, I thought, *I guess you can't cry at grief support groups.* I never went back.

I feel a special empathy for men who are raised to believe that crying is only for sissies and who try desperately to live up to this meaningless measure of manhood. I mean, when it's only minimally acceptable that I, a woman, cry, what are the pressures put on men? I don't even want to think about how hard that is!

So if you can't stand the tears, slip out of line and let someone get in your place who does know how to let someone cry.

21.
Don't say, "God (or Buddha, Mother Nature, Allah, the Universe, or the Great Pumpkin) never gives us more than we can handle"

What the bereaved won't say out loud: "Boy, have they overestimated me!"

Ah, yes, my personal favorite because it's so devastatingly wrong on two levels. First, I find it impossible to accept that my concept of a significant religious other "gives" me pain, cancer, car accidents, or murders just to test my mettle. We'll undoubtedly debate the issue for several more centuries, but I'm standing firm. God didn't give my son cancer to test my strength. And really, what kind of supreme being would make my son suffer just to see how strong I am?

Second, let's assume for a moment that the vengeful supreme being contingent is right. We never get more than we can handle? Well, if true, She's severely overestimated me and every other parent who has lost a child, every widow who has lost her husband, and every widower who has lost his wife. The untimely death of a loved one can't be handled. No one survives it. There's no recovering from it. Simply, what happens is that we get more used to the pain. We take life not one day at a time but one step at a time.

The grain of truth in this atrocious statement is that society forces the bereaved to behave as though they're OK, to look like they've recovered. It's called Academy Award recovery. Don't believe it. It's all an act. Don't stop helping the bereaved because they appear to be doing fine, and don't guilt-trip them into appearing that way when they're not fine (see Tip #70).

22.
Don't say, "You need to get on with your life"

What the bereaved won't say out loud: "Yeah, and I bet you have the answer to world peace, too!"

The most important thing to remember is that the bereaved

can't just jump up and get on with their lives. The lives they planned on living are gone forever. They have to create new ones that they build around the holes left by their loss—lives that they can somehow convince themselves have as much meaning without their loved one as with them.

This takes time. Grief has no set timetable. Even the ground-breaking work of Elisabeth Kübler-Ross in defining the stages of grief gives no time limit for the bereaved to pass through them. And the stages don't occur linearly. They're circular. Just when the bereaved think they've got the anger stage under control and can move on to acceptance, some trigger sends them back into denial or a repeat of the initial shock.

I'll let you in on a secret. It's been fifteen years since my son's death, and writing this chapter brought up so many anger issues, issues I thought were behind me, that it took a month to write it. It's only twelve pages.

Well, excuse me for a minute before I go on to chapter 3. I'm printing out a list of the Atrocious Eleven never to say to the bereaved, and I'm going outside to do a ritual burning. I hope you'll remember never to say them.

3

WHEN THE BEREAVED IS A FRIEND WHO SHARES A COMMON INTEREST

This chapter is for all you folks who know the bereaved because he's your fourth partner at golf; she plays bridge with you; he is studying music with you in an adult-ed class; she teaches you quilting, car maintenance, sailing knots, or bread making; or he attends religious services with you. You've never become really close friends with the bereaved, but you'd like to do something to help in her time of need without overwhelming her with a gesture that's too strong or inappropriate. Let's get started!

23.
Be proactive!

The bereaved, just like the rest of us, doesn't want to be a burden to anyone by asking for help. He isn't going to call you. You have to take the first step, be proactive, and call them. A woman I interviewed told me that a close friend of hers said, "Next time you're in town, call me and I'll take you to dinner." The woman was hurt. Why? She felt her friend should have set a date for the dinner, offered to pick her up, come to visit her. This woman felt her friend had left the onus on her to connect when it was she who needed to be connected to. She hasn't spoken with this friend since and feels heavy guilt because of it.

Give some thought to your first contact after the funeral. Don't be miffed if the bereaved doesn't jump for joy just because you called. I know that sounds contradictory to the advice in the previous paragraph, but special allowances need to be extended to the bereaved. He's still in shock, in mourning— still not up to making decisions or feeling anything other than pain. Don't take it personally if the bereaved refuses your first invitation. Try to talk for a while and then retreat. Remain proactive and call again in the future.

24.

Tuck a book of stamps in with that sympathy card

A friend who grew up in the Midwest told me that people in her area put postage stamps in their sympathy cards. I think this is a great idea. If you haven't been through a loss yet, you don't realize how many thank-you cards must be sent: for flowers at the funeral home, the house, or the gravesite; for food brought to the house for the family or for the reception after the funeral; for Mass cards, trees planted in Israel, and donations to the cancer society; to hospice or to favorite charities that people gave to in remembrance of the deceased.

When you have to write them out, it seems there are thousands of thank-you cards to send. And then you realize you're out of stamps. Having a couple of books of stamps on hand means one less trip out of the house because, as you'll read in Tip #28, coming home to an empty house is challenging for the bereaved.

25.
Plan a playdate

If you know the bereaved because you belong to the same club, play the same sport, or go to the same church, plan an afternoon of activities that relate to your shared interest. Quilters, for instance, love fabric stores. Find a new one to go to, perhaps in another city. Make all the plans, and then invite your friend to go along. For golfers, how about eighteen holes, just the two of you, with a stop at the clubhouse for drinks and dinner? A movie buff might like someone to go with to see the latest Oscar nominee at the movie theater.

Whatever playdate you plan, make sure you aren't taking the bereaved to a spot that was a favorite haunt with the deceased. New and different is what's called for here. You don't want to rip open that partially healed heart by taking the bereaved to a favorite restaurant!

Make all the plans before you invite the bereaved. It's easier to go out if someone else has made all the decisions. The bereaved have enough decisions to make without planning entertainment as well.

Explain what you have in mind, tell him that you'll drive, and ask, please, please, please, won't he come with you? Tell him you really don't want to go alone. (Sometimes deviousness is required!)

26.
Visit the bereaved at home

You can do or discuss whatever hobby, avocation, or interest brought you together in a visit to the bereaved's home. In the weeks immediately following the funeral, your friend may not be ready to go out. So go to your friend. Quilt together, watch a movie, talk books or politics, gossip about the famous, regale your friend with the stupid bids at the latest bridge-club meeting. Bring dinner, and stay to eat it.

27.
Educate the people in your club or organization about grief

Up to now it's been just you and the bereaved interacting, with you doing all the work. Getting tired? You should be! Now's the time to include a few other of your cohorts along to share the load. There are more people than the bereaved who share your interest. Enlist them in "Operation Help." There are four for golf, four for bridge, a dozen or more for quilt group, and an entire congregation at church.

After you call and offer to pick up and drive your friend to the meeting or gathering, call the rest of the members of your group and alert them that the bereaved will attend your next meeting. Bring them up to date on his situation, mood, and progress. Tell them to act normally. If this will be the first time some of the members have seen him since the loss, explain that condolences are acceptable but that they should get back to treating him as they always did at meetings. Remind them they can't catch death from hanging out with the bereaved, and they shouldn't ignore him. This is not the time to press their fears or lack of confidence on the bereaved. Tell them to suck it up and act normally, even if the bereaved seems slightly distracted and less outgoing than before the loss.

This is so important that I'll repeat it here and will probably repeat it again in future chapters: don't treat the bereaved differently than you did before the loss. Yeah, he's changed. Who wouldn't have? But basically he's the same person he always was, and he deserves to be treated as you always treated him. Resist the all-too-human urge to avoid him.

28.

Arrange to be an escort to your next meeting or event

This is an excellent way to ease your friend back into the hobby, sport, or interest that got you together in the first place. Call and let your friend know that there's a meeting coming up with a great speaker, or that your golfing buddies are trying out a new course, or that there's a quilt show in town or a Scrabble tournament she might enjoy. If your friend sounds interested, state that you'd like to pick her up and take her to the event. If your friend agrees, congratulations! You've made an important first step in helping. Now here's what you do.

Show up at your friend's door a few minutes before the agreed-upon time. And I mean that literally. Go up to the door, knock, ring the bell, go in if you're invited to or if your friend isn't quite ready. This helps allay those going-out jitters that might be settling in on the bereaved.

Make conversation on the way to the event, but don't be surprised if you do all the talking. Definitely ask how your friend is doing, and if she's adjusting yet to the changes in her life. If you get one-word answers, switch the topic to a safer area, such as discussing the event you're headed to.

While at the event, make sure your friend is never an island or standing alone. You don't have to hover or join her at the hip; just be there. Most likely the other people she's met through your shared interest will speak with her, too. But if you turn around and notice she's alone, sidle on up and ask if she liked the speaker or quilting or Scrabble.

Now comes the really important part. You do deserve a pat on the back for getting your friend out of the house to be with people. When you drive her home, don't just drop her off with your car running. Park, walk her to the door, make sure she gets inside OK, and if you can, go into the house with her. Going out, while difficult for the bereaved, is nowhere near as hard as coming home to an empty house, especially if her deceased loved one lived there with her. Walking in the door and hearing the echoes of absence, and the slap in the face that follows when she remembers no one is there to greet her, is as bad as when she first learned of the loss. Many a time I stayed home just so I wouldn't have to walk back into that empty house. Then a friend walked me to my door and came in with me for a few minutes after a quilt group meeting, and coming home was a little easier. I learned after that to ask my escort to walk me to my door and come in to chat for just a minute or two. It worked wonders.

29.

Offer to do all the work to hold a meeting of your group at his home

This works especially well for groups that rotate meetings at members' homes. But don't be too quick to suggest this. It may take several week, or more likely, months for your club member to face the prospect of a meeting. Let some time pass before suggesting it. But if several months have passed and he hasn't attended any meetings at all, it's time to offer to bring the mountain to Muhammad, especially if your group met at the bereaved's home before the loss.

Call and ask to hold the next meeting there: "Oh, everyone misses that inebriated goldfish of yours! We'll bring everything—can we have the meeting there?" This suggestion has the added benefit of bringing more people into the current life of the bereaved and into a home empty of other voices for too long.

30.
Be careful what you offer—the septic tank might be full!

I don't know how many times I've heard, "If there's anything I can do to help, just ask." Even worse, before I became knowledgeable of such things the hard way, I don't know how many times I said it to someone else. Again, this statement is one of the things we think of as being helpful to the bereaved. It isn't, and here's a story that shows why.

About ten years after losing my son, I attended an evening workshop on how to get through the holidays. Holidays, especially the ones in the first year after a loss, are difficult for the bereaved. It wasn't the first Christmas without my son, but I felt the need for a refresher course, so I attended. There were two facilitators, each with enough credentials in social work, psychology, or grief counseling to drown us in alphabet soup. After some preliminary information about the difficulty of the bereaved in asking for help, an attendee volunteered to participate in a role-playing experiment. It went something like this:

FACILITATOR: I was so sorry to hear about the death of your husband. How are you doing?

VOLUNTEER: Oh, I'm fine.

FACILITATOR: That's wonderful! But it must be hard. How are you dealing with it?

VOLUNTEER: Well, I just—I try. (She shrugs.)

FACILITATOR *(very kindly)*: You don't really want to talk about it, do you?

VOLUNTEER: No. No, I don't.

FACILITATOR: I understand. Please remember, though, that I'm here if you need me. Anything I can do to help, please just ask. *(Several long seconds of silence.)*

VOLUNTEER: Hmm…I do need some help cleaning my house.

FACILITATOR *(laughing)*: Well, I'm not going to do *that*!

Everyone except the volunteer and me laughed along with the facilitator. I sat, distraught, hurt, and seething, through two more role-playing segments without hearing them, before I had the courage to timidly raise my hand and make my complaint.

ME: You should have immediately said yes, that you'd help clean her house and set up a time. (I saw the volunteer, back in the audience, nodding.) Why didn't you?

FACILITATOR: Well, cleaning someone's house is, well—it's a little too private.

ME: But you offered to do anything. Wouldn't that include cleaning the house if that's what she needed done?

You see, I remembered those early days of bereavement when a good day was being able to get out of bed. A better day was being able to get out of bed and get dressed. It was weeks before cleaning house made it to the good-day list. Even when I got back to it, cleaning house was a slipshod, only-the-basics, who-cares-anyway endeavor. The role play showed me two things. First, I should have asked for help cleaning the house. Second, if people offer to do anything to help, they better be willing and able to do anything that gets asked!

Forget the vague, open-ended pronouncement, "Anything you need, just ask." It's no shame to not want to clean someone else's house. I still don't want to clean my own, so why would I offer to clean someone else's? But it is a shame to make the offer and then have to refuse. After all, we're not all doctors, lawyers, accountants, housekeepers, taxi drivers, or psychologists. There are simply too many things we can't do to help. Save yourself the guilt and the bereaved the disappointment of a refusal to a request for help.

Instead of the all-encompassing offer, instead ask, "Is there something you need? I'd really like to help. Whatever it is, if I can't do it, I'll find someone who can to help you." Now that, we can deliver.

31.
Read that body language

Knowing when it's OK to hug or touch and when to keep your distance can be difficult. People who are bereaved experience a wide range of emotions, sometimes in the blink of an eye. What grieving people communicate nonverbally is often more important than the words they use to express their ideas or emotions. Learn to read the body language, and learn to send signals yourself that you are interested in helping a grieving friend or family member.

Dr. Michelle Roth Cohen, a Los Angeles psychologist and radio personality specializing in relationships, offers insight into how to recognize signs that tip you off to what a person is really feeling. She identifies closed-body behavior—which includes averting the eyes, leaning away from the person you're talking with, or putting barriers such as crossed arms and legs between you and the other person—as people showing discomfort either with themselves or with others. If the bereaved behaves this way, no matter what he's saying, it's probably not a good time to move in for a hug or a comforting touch, as he will likely feel that it is an aggressive move on your part.

On the other hand, open-body behavior conveys a completely different thing. If the bereaved ignores distractions, makes direct eye contact, and sits still, you have a good indication that there are no barriers between you and that person during your conversation. Another positive signal is that the person inclines slightly in your direction, maybe tilting his or her head toward you and nodding. If this is what you see, you can safely move closer or put an arm around the bereaved to offer comfort.

Something else to consider is whether the bereaved is a man or woman. Everybody's grief is unique, certainly, but there are some gender-conditioning issues that can arise and cause problems. The social taboo against male tears can wreak havoc with a man's ability to express his grief or to accept nonsexual touching as comforting. Also, men are expected to be tough and strong—exactly what grieving people feel they aren't. They may be exhibiting a defensiveness they don't really feel. Before you intrude on a man's personal space with an unwelcome embrace, tell the man you feel like hugging him, and ask him whether he would mind if you did.

Women, on the other hand, have more flexibility in our society when it comes to accepting embraces. However, before you move to hug or touch a grieving woman, double-check that the nonverbal signals she's transmitting are positive ones.

Remember, too, that body language is something you send and receive. When you are in the company of a person who is grieving, pay particular attention to how you hold up your end of the nonverbal conversation. Even if you say, "I am here for you," if you are sitting hunched down, arms folded over, and your chin tucked into your chest, the message you deliver is a resounding, "Get away from me." If you pace around the room, perch on the edge of a chair, or jiggle your legs, you're signaling, "Get me out of here." The last thing the bereaved wants is to make the people around him feel uncomfortable or like they need to escape. And you don't want to make the bereaved feel those things, either.

Dr. Roth Cohen says, "You always have to take into consideration the context and the situation that people are presenting in their body language. So you can never assume anything."

32.
Shut up and listen

OK, stop trembling. I can feel your hands shaking through the binding of this book. As a casual friend of the bereaved who shares a hobby or interest, you're not liable to be the first line of defense when the bereaved is ready to bare his soul and pain over the loss of a loved one. This doesn't mean you shouldn't be ready to listen if he opens up to you. Something about you has signaled that you're trustworthy for a confidence or two. How should you handle it?

Beyond asking him how he's doing, I don't advise that you probe too deeply into his mood, feelings, or healing accomplishments. That's for people with closer relationships to him than you have. But if he does open up, go back and reread Tip #1.

You can't fix it, so don't try. Don't offer other examples of what someone else you know did in a similar situation. This person's experience is unique. If I've learned anything from bereavement, it's that we all grieve differently. Just because something worked for someone else doesn't mean it'll work universally. Don't offer advice unless asked. If you are asked for advice and can't come up with anything relevant, it's OK to say you don't know. It's also OK to offer to ask someone else who might know.

If the bereaved opens up to you, it's best to just listen. Let him talk; it's what he needs to do. Bereaved people need to talk about their experiences. It's a major component of healing. Finding people who are willing to listen is the hard part.

Don't play the hero. Nod frequently. Agree frequently. Be encouragingly silent. Listen.

4

WHEN THE BEREAVED IS YOUR CO-WORKER

We spend roughly a third of our lives at work. In that much time we're sure to have some fairly strong relationships with our co-workers. Sometimes these friendships extend outside our workday. It's more likely, though, that the relationship stays within the bounds of the workplace. This doesn't mean that we don't share our lives with the people at work. I value the advice, friendship, and help I've received over the years from the people I work with.

It's his job that will define how much time the bereaved has to adjust to the shock of a loss. Typically, three paid bereavement days is company policy for someone who's lost a close family member. Anyone who's been through this knows that may not be enough. Some people prefer to dive right back into work after a loss. It helps them. Others, like me, need more time away from work. The Family Medical Leave Act (FMLA) offers an employee job protection when a family member is seriously ill and needs the employee at home to care for him or her. The employee may need months off to care for a loved one. But the

FMLA does not provide job protection to cover a bereavement period if that family member dies. Your company may offer a leave-of-absence policy that will hold the bereaved's job for a certain amount of time to grieve. Most often the employee's accumulated vacation or sick time must supplement such a leave. Finances may dictate that the bereaved return to work immediately to keep his head above rising financial waters. Whether your co-worker returns right after the three-day bereavement period or is out for a month or more, he'll need help from his entire team at work.

33.
Offer to be the workplace newscaster

Although we discussed in the previous chapter the importance of human contact, I don't recommend that all five, ten, or twenty members of the workplace team call the bereaved individually during the time he's out of work. Offer to be the newscaster. You, and only you, will call the bereaved once or twice a week—whatever's appropriate—to find out how your co-worker is holding up and to offer assistance. Newscasting works both ways. Fill him in on what's happening at work so he's somewhat up to speed when he returns. Perhaps a planned computer upgrade was rescheduled or a new policy instituted. If changes at work affect his job, let him know so he isn't surprised when he gets back.

Ask him how he's doing and if he needs help with something. He might need a form from human resources or to return a completed form. Set up a time and place to complete that task for him. Let him know of any employee events on the horizon. Maybe he'll attempt to attend them even though he's not at work. Make sure you tell him everyone's thinking of him and hoping he's OK.

Then update your team at work. Tell them how he said he's feeling and how he sounded. Pass on any requests for help and find someone to fulfill them. Make sure you share with them any greetings or information he passed on to you.

Also update his supervisor on how he's doing, but don't make any back-to-work commitments on his behalf unless he's instructed you to do so. And don't get caught in the trap of being the boss's mole. If supervisors need to know something, they should call him directly, not use you as an intermediary for personnel or solely work-related information.

34.

Don't push her to come back to work too soon

Make sure you tell your bereaved co-worker that keeping in touch is not a way to make her come back to work sooner. Explain that there are no ulterior motives for your phone calls other than helping her get through a difficult time. So it follows that your phone calls are not the time to whine about how behind the department is, how much more work you've had to take on, or that all the other employees are overworked, overstressed, and could use a vacation, too. Your co-worker is not on vacation. She's healing. Don't load a pile of guilt on her, and think about what you say beforehand so you don't do so unintentionally. End the phone call with the sentiment that, while the whole department misses her, everyone wants her to be ready when she comes back, and she shouldn't attempt to return until she feels truly ready.

35.
Offer to take on a task

Whether your colleague is out for several weeks or months or returns to work immediately, he'll need on-the-job help both now and when he gets back. It's a unique personality that can get right back on the job to perform at the same speed, quantity, and quality as he did before a loss. It might be a welcome gesture to offer to take over one of his tasks for awhile. If several co-workers offer this, all the work gets done on time without overburdening anyone on the team and still giving the bereaved some breathing room.

Definitely clear this with his supervisor and yours before you make the offer. It's probable your supervisor or employer would be happy to agree in advance. But don't make it a surprise, and don't go ahead and do it behind a supervisor's back. And don't offer it to the bereaved until you have permission to do so.

What if the bereaved co-worker is your supervisor? All the same suggestions apply here, too. Additionally, offer to fill the supervisor's shoes, even on a rotating basis, while she's out. If the company decides to bring someone in to take over your supervisor's duties while she's out, be considerate and helpful. Keep an eye out for how you can make the replacement's job easier by explaining department policy and procedures. Be supportive.

36.
Don't dump those tasks on her desk on her first day back at work

---

Yep, I get it. You're overworked, and you're tired. The temptation to clear your desk of tasks that aren't yours is strong. Resist it. Dumping everything back on the bereaved's desk on her first day back is like burying her in an avalanche. True, she might be ready to handle it, but it wouldn't hurt to ask her when she'd be able to take the task back and say that you're willing to set aside the required time to bring her back up to speed on what's been happening with that task.

If your supervisor doesn't suggest it, request a staff meeting as soon as you know a start-back date for your co-worker. During the meeting, create a plan to bring her up to date with the department, and decide how many tasks she should be given back on her first day and how many can stay in others' hands for a week or two. Remember, the bereaved doesn't want to be a bother to anyone. If she's asked if she can take everything back on her first day, she's apt to say yes, because she knows you've all made sacrifices since she took a bereavement leave. Plan ahead. Things will get back to normal pretty quickly, and that extra work will be off your desk for good. By the way, if everyone involved forgets to say thank you for your sacrifice, I'll say it. You did well. Thanks!

37.
Donate a vacation day

If your colleague is grieving a death after a long illness and has used up all his vacation and sick time but still needs more days away from work, check with your supervisor or human resources department to ask whether you can donate one of your vacation days to the bereaved. This is a little tricky. Most people don't ask for this very often. I worked at one nonprofit that allowed us to donate vacation days to a co-worker who took care of her father until he died. She had used up all her own time off with pay but wasn't quite ready to come back to work. She needed the money though, and a bunch of us got together and appealed to the boss to allow us to donate our time.

I spoke with several human resources managers, and they saw the request as a major tracking problem. After all, the rates of hourly pay being donated might be different from the bereaved employee's rate of pay. I suggested that they use the simple expedient of a calculator and the time-honored practice of math. Dividing the amount of one day of donated pay by the bereaved employee's hourly rate will easily reveal how many hours are donated.

More importantly, the managers were concerned that the practice would set a precedent that could cost the company in ways managers hadn't planned on, like increased production time, missed deadlines, and so on, but the goodwill engendered by donations would pay off in employee loyalty and increased morale. I certainly hope companies allow employees to donate time to sick or bereaved co-workers in the future. We can speed up the process by asking our human resources managers to review the policy of doing so. For now, ask, but be prepared that the answer may be no.

There is a way around a no. If your company allows it, ask for a day's vacation pay in advance. Then, tactfully, give it to your colleague. (Maybe you can avoid embarrassing the bereaved by saying you took up a collection at the office. Hmm. Maybe that should be another tip, huh?)

38.
Take up a collection at the office

Of course, this only makes sense if the bereaved is in financial need. If she is, all the flowers, fruit baskets, cards, and phone calls, though appreciated, won't quite cut it. A little cash discreetly given to her might be a godsend to offset expenses until insurance checks arrive or the probate is finalized.

The need for funds is particularly acute in the event of an untimely death. When a parent dies, at least half, if not all, of the family income stops coming. If the deceased left behind underage children, the financial need increases. The need rises exponentially if, God forbid, the deceased was too young to get around to things like obtaining an adequate life insurance policy, contributing to a 401(k), or saving for a rainy day. Often people get together to raise funds for an education trust for the children left behind. Talk up the idea of a trust fund with your co-workers, get a committee together, and get to work. You won't feel frustratingly helpless when you participate in such an important aid to the bereaved.

39.
Set up the trust fund the right way

The concept of a trust fund, set up from donations, for children who've lost one or both parents isn't a new one. But it can become a complicated process, requiring consultations with lawyers and probate judges. There are so many variables in helping children who've lost a parent that I strongly recommend that you coordinate your efforts with the surviving parent or appointed guardian, the family's lawyer, and the probate office. This is why in Tip #38 I recommend that you set up a committee to work together on this. One person may find it to be a daunting task.

I'm no lawyer and won't pretend to be. The following is just a broad overview of what you can do to help the surviving children. I spoke with Michael A. Goncalves, vice-president and senior financial consultant for Webster Bank Investments. Michael just happens to spend two days a week in my local Webster branch and would be the person I'd go to first when investigating the *do*s and *don't*s of setting up an education trust fund. Your bank branch has a person just like Michael on staff to help you.

Michael began our interview by listing the plethora of ways that creating a trust for children is fraught with legal concerns. "I'm no lawyer," said Michael right off the bat (where have you heard that before?), "and I'm not giving legal advice. So many things come into play for this." Michael went on to list examples: families with assets, families with no assets, families with one surviving parent, families with no surviving parent, probate, financial condition at the time of the loss, custody issues, and on and on and on. Poor Michael was quick to point out that he wasn't the first person to go to for information on this topic; usually people speak to a financial planner or lawyer first. Michael also pointed out that most banks would definitely not get involved in running any fund-raisers or donation campaigns. Your bank and your bank's financial adviser would enter the picture only when all the other details, such as naming the trustees, are worked out. Even then, all the bank does is advise you on the best possible way to invest the money you've collected. But I still wanted to give you some information on what you can do to help. So I described a strictly fictional scenario that Michael could address comfortably.

The primary breadwinner in the family is the lost loved one. The deceased parent was very young, and there was no life insurance provision for the family. The surviving parent works, but the salary will cover only house and car payments, food, and clothing—in short, the necessities. It will be a while before the surviving parent can afford to save any significant amount. Friends, co-workers, and neighbors put together an effort to raise money for the children's education. They've cleared all the financial, legal, custodial, and probate hurdles. What do they do with the money?

"In that case, a 529 savings plan is the way to go," said Michael. "Every state has at least one 529 savings plan offering." Michael explained that there was information on the Internet that explained, compared, rated, and evaluated various 529 plans. So I surfed the Internet and found www.savingforcollege.com. It's not the only site on the Internet that covers this topic, but I was impressed and reassured that the site earned its income from targeted advertising and not from charging visitors membership or consulting fees. Its founder Joseph Hurley has a mission statement that stresses providing site visitors with objective information on 529 plans. A 529 plan is a tax-free savings plan for postsecondary education: bachelor's, graduate, and advanced degrees like medicine or business. Usually parents set it up and own it, but name a child as the account beneficiary. Some states require that the money saved is used at an in-state college or university. Other states allow 529 savings plan money from another state to apply to an educational institution in that state, but at a reduced rate. The permutations of what states allow are endless. The major offerings of the website were its information on each state's requirements, a comparison of their annual fees, and a rating system. The site does offer for sale two books on how to get the most out of 529 education plans, and there are at least a dozen more available through online and local bookstores.

OK, so all this sounds daunting. That's why I suggested getting a committee together, remember? And the sense of accomplishment, the pride in doing something significant, reduces the feelings of helplessness we all feel after someone we know loses a loved one. Be persistent, be dogged, be downright aggressive, and get it done. You'll have done something truly lasting to show you care.

40.

Managers, inform and support your employee regarding the company's leave policy

---

Your staff got together and picked a newscaster to keep in touch with their bereaved co-worker. The newscaster is keeping her informed on happenings in the office, asking what she needs done, and forwarding information to the rest of her co-workers.

But that doesn't let you off the hook. You should add her home email to any department-wide notices. And you have the responsibility of keeping her informed on the company's policy on leaves such as the one she's taking. That might be the hardest part of your job, depending on the latitude your supervisors and the company policy allow you. No one in the company, especially you, wants to lose a valuable employee. Be her champion with the higher-ups if that becomes necessary. Remember to compliment the rest of your staff for making the effort to stay on track and deliver on deadline even though they're a person short. C'mon, you can do that! You know how much one kind word can do to improve morale. Try it. You'll like the results.

41.
Managers, educate your staff about grief and bereavement

I read about the suggestion to educate staff in an article titled "Danger: Grief at Work," written by Dr. Bill Webster, a grief counselor, author, and founder of www.griefjourney.com.

Webster wrote, "Some ideas for the business manager: organize lunchtime seminars for interested staff and employees; access community support groups often available through local funeral homes; offer bereavement counseling resources; and offer training workshops for staff on understanding grief and support for grieving employees."

Many companies today offer employee assistance programs (EAPs), which are free assessment and counseling services for employees that began in the 1970s as a way to reduce loss of productivity due to employee drug or substance abuse problems. Today, EAPs cover a wide range of employee problems that affect productivity; bereavement is one of them. According to CorpCare, one of the largest national providers of EAP services in the country, company productivity can decrease 2 percent solely from problems associated with grief. Companies that provide EAP services report lower incidences of absenteeism, tardiness, and sick leave.

Offering some sort of grief education in the workplace is a highly proactive move on management's part to train workers on how to treat a bereaved co-worker so that there is as little disruption in productivity as possible. By using your company's EAP or resources available from local hospitals, mental health centers, or funeral homes, all employees benefit, but your production and your employer just might benefit the most.

42.

Work to change the Family Medical Leave Act to include the bereaved

As noted earlier, the Family Medical Leave Act (FMLA) protects an employee's job while the employee cares for a family member's illness, or his or her own illness. But it doesn't offer the same protection for bereavement. I believe that this is a terrible gap in the law. We can change that. Place a call, send an email, or post a letter to your senators and representatives. Tell them that we need time for grieving if a family member we've been caring for happens to die. Because many states also have FMLA provisions in state statutes, copy your communication to your governor, local department of labor, and state representative. Let's get the ball rolling on this issue!

43.

Don't dump on the boss or the company for policies currently in place

You won't make any points or help the atmosphere surrounding your bereaved co-worker by bad-mouthing the boss or the company for its current bereavement policies. Sure, you think those policies are outdated and inadequate. And, yes, you're indignant over the lack of empathy shown to your co-worker.

But complaining loudly, or even softly, at lunch, on breaks, and in the hallways won't get you one step closer to what you want. In fact, your behavior may intensify the tension in your workplace. You have two options.

First, you can work for change instead of just complaining about it. Check out your company's policies for employee input on benefits and workplace procedures. If there's wording on how to present a request to management, follow those steps to bring your suggestion for a better bereavement policy to management. Use the bibliography and Web resources in the back of this book to find sources for statistics and examples that prove that the change will benefit the company as well as the employee.

Your second option? Find a company that does offer a bereavement policy you feel is adequate and set a goal to find a job at that company. I realize this one's not so easy. You may have a wonderful job at your present company, excepting its outdated bereavement policy. Weigh the benefits you do have and then decide whether you can stay or search, carefully, for another job.

Whichever option you choose, actions speak louder than words. Don't just complain. Be proactive and do something!

44.

She's not different; she's just sad

Treat the bereaved as normally as you possibly can. Don't walk on tiptoes around your co-worker. Try to make work time the same as it's always been. A common complaint from the bereaved is that everyone treats them too specially. Yes, she's probably quieter than she used to be, and a little shier and withdrawn. She's still figuring out how to live a new life and doesn't know what to do or say any more than you do. It's a gray area, to be sure, walking the line between being sensitive to her needs and keeping the office humming like always. There are deadlines to meet, projects to finish, decisions to make, jokes to tell, politics to discuss, and social things happening as well. Include your colleague in coffee breaks, lunch, and office chat. Share that joke with her, too. She still knows how to laugh at a good joke. If your co-workers occasionally go out together after work for a drink or dinner, do it a little more often and always invite your colleague to join in.

While you work hard not to treat her too specially, be sure that you aren't avoiding her either. Another sadness heaped on the bereaved is that her friends, co-workers, and even family are so worried about saying the wrong thing or not knowing what to do that they avoid their bereaved friend. The bereaved knows, by hard experience, that the best way to clear a room is to tell someone she's just lost a loved one. Within minutes, excuses fill the air, and the group she was talking with has separated and escaped to other conversation groups. We learn early, the bereaved, that if the people we're with don't know our history, we keep it a secret. I still make it a policy, fifteen years after losing my son, never to mention my tragic loss to strangers. Often, I'm asked whether I have children. As much as I'd love to share stories about my son and motherhood, I always say no and lead the conversation on to other topics.

45.
By gosh, don't gush!

OK, so this is simply a variation on shut up and listen. Listening is so important that it bears repeating. When your bereaved co-worker returns to work, don't gush over him. Don't babble on with condolences that serve only to make both you and the bereaved uncomfortable. A simple "I'm so sorry for your loss" is sufficient. Don't expect him to gush in return either. The circumstances of how the loss occurred are personal, and your co-worker may want to keep them private. Respect this and don't push for information. Move immediately to work topics, and offer to get him settled in and brought back up to date.

There may come a time that your co-worker does want to talk. Talking about the person who is gone or the circumstances that took that person are part of the grieving process. The more times that a bereaved person can share his story with a good listener, the more completely he'll grieve and adapt. You'll know when he's ready to talk. On one of your regular daily stops at his desk to check in on how he's doing, he might stop working, make eye contact, and tell you how he's really feeling. He may have decided that he trusts you not to judge him or present him with a list of things he should do. So, shut up and listen. Pull up a chair if that seems appropriate. You'll want to balance your need to help him and his need to be helped with getting your work done on the job. If the conversation lasts too long or both of your emotions start taking over, you can gently suggest that you'd be happy to continue the conversation at lunch or after work over coffee. Remember, you're at work. Don't be rude. Be gentle.

Conversely, you'll also know if he's not ready to talk. You stop by his desk and ask how it's going and you get a one-word answer: "Fine." He keeps working and won't make eye contact with you. Don't be offended, and don't take it personally. The bereaved are more confused than you about what to do and what to say. If the time isn't right for a conversation, you'll know it. Ask if there's anything job related that you can help with. If he refuses your offer, and odds are he will, move on. Take the Scarlett O'Hara approach to life: tomorrow is another day.

5

WHEN THE BEREAVED IS YOUR NEIGHBOR

Your neighbors are the folks who live next door or down the street. Your kids grew up with their kids. You've picnicked at their house, and they've partied at yours. When he broke his leg, you went and mowed the lawn. When she was sick with the flu, you watched the kids, checked up on her, drove to the drugstore for medicine. Well, the loss of a loved one is no different from any of the other problems you've helped your neighbor through except that it's sadder and the aftereffects last longer.

46.

Understand the effects of our culture on the bereaved's ability to grieve

---

As a neighbor and friend, your ear is likely more available to the bereaved than that of a club member or co-worker (where time spent talking about anything but work is often discouraged), but the bereaved's beliefs about what is OK or not OK to do in front of others may influence how she will behave with you.

As noted in the introduction, death has surpassed sex as the number-one taboo subject—both publicly and privately! Add that crying in public is another strict taboo and the bereaved is left with two choices: isolate herself and stay away from people, or put on her Academy Award–winning "all better" face and lock the pain inside. While both approaches are sometimes required, as permanent habits they create more problems than they solve. Grief is stressful, and people who don't grieve when they need to (because they think others will judge them as wimps) will pay for it later. That unrelieved stress will come out—usually in the form of a physical or mental illness.

Fear of being judged as too emotional and making the listener uncomfortable is, and was for me, the reason that those of you willing to listen will have a hard time getting the bereaved to talk. Be patient. Be gently persistent. Make it known, repeatedly, that you believe grief takes time. That everyone grieves differently. And, most of all, that as a neighbor and friend, you're there for the duration.

47.
Give him the gift of time

"Well, thank God that's over," we say as we return home or to work after a funeral. Our sense of relief is palpable. We redirect our thoughts to happier things, our hands to more productive activities. Ah, yes, life can get back to normal now. Not totally callous or unsympathetic, you may even tap a note into your Blackberry to call and set up dinner with the bereaved for next week. That'll be good. Get him out of the house. Get some good food in him and a few laughs. It'll be fun. It always was before.

You're knocked off your feet when you call with your invitation and he refuses. He doesn't want to go out to dinner. *What's the matter with him?* you might think. *The funeral's over. It's been a week. Why isn't he getting back to his life?*

Because a week obviously isn't enough for him. Those of us who didn't live with or have daily contact with the deceased don't realize that there is no life as our friend knew it to go back to. Everything is different. An important component of his life is gone, and nothing will be the same again. The bereaved must re-create a life around the hole left by the deceased person's absence. There is no deadline for the end of grief. Give your neighbor the weeks, months, years, or even decades that it takes to adapt to a new way of life. The bad news is that the bereaved never recovers from the loss of a loved one. The pain never goes away. I can't say this enough: the bereaved just gets more used to it and gradually functions again. The gift of time. Ah, now you've got it. There's no gift more priceless.

48.
Allow her to grieve her way

Along with giving her the gift of time, give her the gift of allowing her to be herself. Everyone grieves differently. Some can get back in the saddle of life almost immediately. Repeating old routines is healing. Some will never cry; some will never look back. Others appear unable to do anything they did before. They weep seemingly constantly and can't talk enough about their memories. Take your cues from your neighbor. Forget judgments. If you feel she's gone back to work too soon, ask her how she feels about it. Take a look at all the ways to read body language listed in Tip #31. Support her, as she feels comfortable, in adapting to her new life in her way. And if it doesn't work, be there to help pick up the pieces without saying, "I told you so."

49.
Make breakfast for the morning of the funeral

My dear friend Anne Frazier Walradt gave me this tip: "I noticed that while there were plenty of casseroles, sliced meat, rolls, and desserts, no one had thought about breakfast for the day of the funeral," said Anne. "I make a bacon and cheese quiche because it can be eaten hot, warm, or cold and be just as good. I drop it off the night before or in the morning, early, with juice, rolls or bread, and coffee, tea, or hot chocolate. People seem to really appreciate it. I make two double batches because so many people are likely to be at the house. I make one kind with bacon and another…with mushrooms and spinach. And I use throwaway aluminum pans so the family doesn't have to deal with figuring out who owns which dishes and getting them back to the provider. Square or rectangular pieces warm up more evenly in the microwave as people come down for breakfast, so they're better than the pie-shaped ones."

Way to go, Anne! I think it's a great idea, and the quiche is perfect. People suffering from shock need protein. Eggs are a good protein source, are pretty innocuous, are easily digestible, and are light fare that might appeal to the whole family as they prepare for the funeral. During a tragedy, many people are turned off by food, don't experience hunger, or just find the thought of eating nauseating. This will pass, and even if they don't eat it for breakfast, I'll bet when they find that quiche in the fridge later, they'll be tempted. Here is Anne's quiche recipe. Try it out the next time your neighbor needs a helping hand.

ANNE'S QUICKIE QUICHE

3 eggs

½ cup biscuit mix (or a bit more)

½ cup butter (or substitute)

1½ cups milk

¼ teaspoon of salt

Dash of pepper

¼ cup chopped onion (optional)

1 cup shredded Swiss cheese (or cheddar cheese)

½ cup bacon or ham, cut into small pieces (you can fry the bacon first for a lower-fat quiche)

Place all ingredients except cheese and meat in a blender and mix for a few seconds to blend well. Pour into a greased 8- or 9-inch square aluminum pan or a pie pan. Sprinkle cheese and meat over the top, and push gently below the surface with the back of a spoon. Bake at 350 degrees for 45 minutes. Allow to set for 10 minutes before serving. If you cook it the day before (which is easiest), refrigerate overnight so others can microwave it in the morning.

Many variations of this recipe exist. Some can be found at www.bettycrocker.com or you can search for "impossible pie" on Google. It's called impossible pie because it makes its own crust—no rolling out the dough. Choose one that sounds like it'd be good for breakfast.

50.
Food, herbs, and other natural remedies that help

As yummy as quiche might sound to you, no appetite, a poor

appetite, or a chaotic appetite are all common for the bereaved. Fatigue sets in. Healthy reserves of vitamins and minerals get depleted. The immune system is compromised. Not a good picture.

I asked Sue Gebo, a consulting nutritionist in private practice in West Hartford, Connecticut, for advice. She gave me several suggestions:

- **Pasta.** There's a reason that we think of pasta as a comfort food. It's not only easy to cook, but it's also delicious and boosts serotonin, a feel-good neurotransmitter.

- **Fruit and salad.** A small bowl of fruit and a bowl of tossed salad are good, healthy choices. Someone who is grieving doesn't have the energy to scrutinize produce or even think about food preparation: too much peeling and too much chopping.

- **Walnuts.** Walnuts are a great source of omega-3 fatty acids, which are known to alleviate depression.

- **Dairy products.** Dairy products are a good source of protein and contain the amino acid tryptophan, which works to allow the brain to release serotonin, that feel-good neurotransmitter. Rather than bring over a gallon of milk, pick up an assortment of single-serving yogurts. When you're thinking about dairy, don't forget pudding. Rice, tapioca, and good old-fashioned chocolate are all good choices.

Here's another tip—one you might not have considered. It comes from Sue's own personal experience. Instead of dropping off all that pasta, fruit, salad, nuts, and pudding—and let's not forget the requisite casseroles, cakes, and sandwiches—tell the bereaved that you brought breakfast, lunch, or dinner "for us." And tell her you're hungry! Your neighbor is less likely to refuse eating if it means you'd be deprived, too.

Finally, don't bring alcohol. We live in a society that readily turns to alcohol as a coping mechanism. Although its numbing effect might provide short-term relief, grief doesn't really drown in a bottle. It comes back—in this case, with a hangover.

Here's a tip for those of you who also like to use herbal and other natural remedies. My friend who is an herbalist and aesthetician, Laurie Neronha (www.viriditasbeauty.com), recommends Bach's Rescue Remedy, a flower essence formula used primarily to ease shock and trauma in the emotional body. "When a person is grieving, he'll walk around like a zombie. That's because the physical body and the emotional body have been traumatized. Rescue Remedy helps to alleviate the emotional shock. It allows the bereaved to assimilate the impact of death in a calm and focused way, a necessary step for healing. A few drops under the tongue will ease the spirit and allow the bereaved to take a good, deep breath. Bach's Rescue Remedy is appropriate for immediate, short-term use and may be used for several weeks if necessary. It is readily available at most health food stores."

The plant world offers additional aids. As Laurie explained, "Flower essences have a profound effect. In general, the heavy, dark, depressed state of grieving is categorized as cold-damp. Crying on the inside. For those who are grieving, any 'sunny' plant, such as dandelion, goldenrod, or calendula, can be used to bring in joy and light. Tinctures of these plants are available at any good health food store. Recommended dosage for the grieving would be two to three drops, three times a day." And all these years, I've been pulling up the dandelions. Who knew?

Referring to her studies with Matthew Wood and his *Book of Herbal Wisdom*, Laurie said that some Native Americans believe in corpse sickness. "If you are touching a person at the moment of death, an electric shock comes from the body of the deceased into the hand of the living. That shock then causes 'wasting.' What follows is the all-too-typical insomnia, anxiety, nervous tension, and lack of appetite. Sure enough, the living appears to waste away. A good remedy? *Monarda fistulosa* [wild bergamot]. Sweet leaf. Wood calls this 'one of the primal healing plants of North America.' A good health food store will carry it."

For the depression that clings to the grieving, Laurie recommends Saint John's wort (*Hypericum perforatum*), "particularly for the romantic broken heart. *Wort* is an old German word that means "medicine." The herb comes in many forms—oil, tincture, tea, flower essence. Other choices include lemon balm (*Melissa officianalis*) tea, a gentle, refreshing tonic, and lavender (*Lavendula angustifolia officinalis*) essential oil. Just a whiff of lavender oil raises the spirit and encourages restful sleep. Put five to ten drops—no more—into the bath to relieve tension."

Laurie added, "Therapeutic herbalism is a specialized field. To find a practitioner in your area, check with the American Herbalists Guild (AHG), a nonprofit, educational organization (www.americanherbalistsguild.com). The herbalist will work directly with the bereaved and recommend appropriate helpers from the green world."

As I've mentioned here and elsewhere, help the bereaved by making the appointment and going with her. If you have a qualified herbal practitioners circle in your area (check with the AHG), ask whether they offer fees on a sliding scale. Many do.

51.

Offer to watch the house during the funeral

Maybe this is an urban legend, but I hear it every time there's a funeral. With all the announcements surrounding a death, the deceased's address is usually included in the obituary or funeral arrangements listed in the paper. It's a perfect opportunity, as the story goes, for the unsavory folks in our world to burglarize the home while everyone is at the funeral. No one, except the burglar, wants this to happen. So it's nice to have someone stay at the house so it's occupied and not a target for thieves. It's been my experience that, true or not, the fear of a burglary during the funeral is a very real concern of the bereaved.

If you can, stop by the house a day or two before the funeral to volunteer to house-sit. The bereaved will know you are serious in your offer, and you can then use the opportunity to have him show you around and fill you in on anything you might need to know, such as the security code, whether to let pets out, and so forth. If you can't stop by, then call and volunteer. And if you can get a few things ready for the reception (if it's at the bereaved's home) to follow the funeral, that's a plus.

52.
Offer to care for infants during the funeral

Although I've expressed before that children's participation in funeral rites is a good thing, infants, particularly those of the bereaved, can hinder the grieving process for their parents. The bereaved may feel torn between caring for the infant and being totally free to experience the healing aspects of the funeral rites. It's a nice gesture to offer to babysit infants during the funeral (see Tip #10). Don't be surprised if your offer is refused, however. There's also something wonderfully healing about holding a baby in your arms, and a parent may need to cling to a child as an affirmation of life in the face of death. The gesture, even if refused, will be appreciated.

53.

Say yes when asked to be a pallbearer

OK, so carrying a casket doesn't really appeal to you. Well, it's not on anyone's list of favorites, but only because few people realize what an honor it is. Yes, an honor. Your participation as a pallbearer adds to the significance of the funeral. Choosing you was not done lightly. You were chosen because you are either related to the deceased or the bereaved, or are a good neighbor and friend. Escorting the deceased through the ceremonies makes you part of an honor guard that the bereaved will long remember, as will everyone who attends the funeral rites. It's one of those duties that can turn into a blessing for you as well. As a pallbearer, you are more closely aligned with the march of time, more in the moment than you would be as just an attendee. Think twice before refusing. You may find it a memorable and rewarding experience.

There's another reason to agree to be a pallbearer. Sometimes the deceased, especially those who have died natural deaths of old age, have few or no relatives or friends left who are able to perform the duties of pallbearer. Sure, the funeral home can supply folks to fill in, but if you're asked to participate, it means that there exists some connection between you and the deceased or the bereaved, however slim. It will mean more to the bereaved if you participate than if the honor guard comprises funeral home employees.

You'll know every step of the process ahead of time. The folks running the funeral home will meet with you and the other pallbearers to brief you on what to do, when to do it, and how to do it. They'll describe the church or funeral site to you so you know what to expect. They'll give you the details of the service so you'll know ahead of time when you're needed. They'll tell you the arrangements made for the gravesite rites and what your role is in them. They won't let you make a mistake, miss a cue, or drop the casket. They'll be with you every step of the way to get you ready and encourage and help you.

Say yes.

54.

Speak up first about the deceased at the funeral

So there you are sitting in a pew, sitting in a folding chair in a memorial chapel, or standing at the gravesite. The service leader says the family has requested that anyone who wants to say something about the deceased can do so now. Comments would be welcome, he or she says. As the quiet around you deepens into one of those cavernously uncomfortable silences, your throat goes dry, and you fear the worst. No one is going to say anything! What a disaster!

It's pretty common to be terrified of public speaking, especially of being the first to speak, but it helps to put yourself in the shoes of the bereaved. They really believe people will come forward with wonderful things to say about their loved one. And if no one does?

So get off your duff, stand up, clear your throat, and say something! C'mon, you thought up an anecdote to share with the bereaved when you expressed your condolences before, didn't you? Repeat it now. Speak slowly, clearly, and loudly enough for everyone to hear. Make Stanislavski proud, and act like your knees aren't knocking, like you do this all the time, and like there's nothing to it. Someone else will follow your lead; that person just didn't want to be first. As the next speaker contributes, sit down, and pat yourself on the back. Look what you started!

Not every family asks for comments from funeral attendees. But when they do, go ahead and contribute. You've participated in the bereaved's healing. Isn't that a good thing?

55.
Visit once a week

This doesn't have to be anything elaborate or time consuming. Just drop by. You're a good neighbor and have probably stopped by once in a while to catch up on family news anyway. So pick up the pace a little, and stop by once a week. Chat for a few minutes, or longer if your neighbor seems ready to talk. A quick but well-meant hug, and you're out the door and on to your errands.

56.
While you're there, check things out

You don't have to be obvious about it, but notice whether the house is clean. Is there a lot of clutter? Has the garbage been emptied? Are there dishes in the sink? Ask for something to drink, and offer to get it yourself. That way you can sneak a peek at what's in the fridge.

Sit down and get a conversation going, and then just get up and start doing the dishes, straightening out the pile of newspapers on the couch, folding the laundry dumped in the wing chair. All while you're talking. Your neighbor might halfheartedly protest, but just say something like, "Well, I'm here, it's here, we're having a nice visit, and I get antsy if I just sit for too long. What were you saying about your brother?" Take the garbage out with you when you leave. And the next time you're at the grocery store, pick up some extra milk, juice, fruit, or fresh vegetables, and drop them off at your neighbor's on your way home.

It's these small acts that can mean the most to the bereaved. And these are the tasks he just can't get to himself. The sadness of grief saps energy and motivation. To the bereaved it may seem like too much effort to rinse a dish and put it in the dishwasher, or to fold laundry, or to take out the garbage. Don't be critical—just do it!

57.

Roll up your sleeves, and get to work
on outdoor home maintenance

Taking a simple drive past your neighbor's house gives you all the information you need for this tip. Does the lawn need mowing? Is it January, and the air conditioners are still in the windows? Is it July, and the storm windows are still on? Is there a shutter askew, a shingle loose, a gutter dangling? Is the driveway still buried in snow from last week's blizzard? These are indications that your bereaved neighbor is still too deep in pain to attend to even the simplest home maintenance.

Get the rest of your neighbors together and divvy up the work. You don't have to do it yourself. A visit to your bereaved neighbor may reveal that he or she can afford to have someone do the work but just hasn't had the energy to make the arrangements. Offer to find someone reputable to do what needs doing.

If there isn't ready money to pay outside help, make a few phone calls to your town hall. Many towns and cities have volunteer organizations that help with outdoor home chores that homeowners can't accomplish on their own. Charitable organizations in my hometown offer a Christmas in April volunteer opportunity for just this purpose. Youth organizations in my hometown have kids participate in volunteer work projects. This is a win-win situation. Your neighbor gets needed household chores done, and youths get work experience to add to their résumés. When my best friend's mother became too frail to do her yard work, her children planned an annual dinner at their mom's house and did it for her. Another win-win situation. The family got together for a nice dinner, and their mom got her yard cleaned up. Maybe your neighbors would enjoy a backyard picnic while helping out.

The point is to be creative. Many hands lighten the load; help from outside may be obtained cheaply enough to solve the maintenance problems. There's always a solution if you look for it.

Don't just drive past and do nothing.

58.

Roll up your sleeves, and get to work on inside home maintenance

---

Tip #56 has already advised you to help out, unobtrusively of course, around the house. Sure, doing so involves some sneaking around in the refrigerator and laundry hamper, but what's a little snooping between friends for a good cause, right?

The same is true for some of the heavier cleaning jobs around the house. Perhaps on your last visit you noticed record dust heights, a rug redecorated with cat hairs, windows too dirty to see out of. These are tasks that can't be done with just a little snooping. These jobs need dust rags, a vacuum cleaner, and a couple of bottles of ammonia. Leave your judgments at home. Cleanliness may indeed be next to godliness (or goddessliness, depending on your views), but the bereaved simply may not have the energy or desire to pick up the phone, much less a vacuum.

Get creative here, too. What about a cleaning party? Once everyone begins cleaning, you might be surprised to discover that the bereaved pitches in. She doesn't want to sit in filth. She just has trouble getting started. Having all of you around could be the impetus to get her going, at least for that day.

If a cleaning party is out of the question, then get in touch with your town hall or the charitable organizations in your town to see what services are available for your bereaved neighbor. If money isn't a problem, then a call to a cleaning service may suffice. And while the merry maids clean, drag your neighbor out to lunch and some shopping. You can both enjoy that!

59.
Offer to run an errand

Some things bear much repetition. The bereaved doesn't want to stay in; it's more that once he is out, he doesn't want to come back to an empty house. So, in the days or weeks immediately following a loss, offer to run an errand or two for him. Take those thank-you cards to the post office. Pick up a prescription.

Fill his car with gas. Get the oil changed. Drop off completed forms at his work or the probate office. Pick up a pint of favorite ice cream. Deliver or pick up some dry cleaning.

As I mentioned in Tip #30, offering to run errands is another area where your offer should be specific. The all-encompassing, "Is there anything you need?' will invariably get a negative response, or the request will be for something you can't or don't want to fulfill. But asking specifically about prescriptions, forms, groceries, mail, dry cleaning, or gas for the car may break through the lethargy that is grief, and you'll be able to do something significant.

60.
Be a little pushy

You know (mostly because your kitchen window faces her front door) that your neighbor is not leaving the house. You've offered to do grocery shopping weeks before and got a no. It's time to get a little pushier. Trot over and get a list of things your neighbor needs for the cupboard and fridge. This time, don't take no for an answer. Be gentle but firm. Get a shopping list out of her by asking leading questions: "You don't have any soup. Do you like soup? What kind?" "What's your favorite bread?" "Do you eat bagels or cereal for breakfast?" "I've forgotten. Do you prefer crunchy or smooth peanut butter?" "I remember you always eating Delicious apples. Want some?"

When you have the list, go shopping. Remember to accept any money the bereaved offers toward the groceries. She's not financially broke but emotionally broke. If she can pay her own way, let her. Accepting too much help from you or anyone else may drive her further into isolation. Letting her pay makes her a participant in getting the groceries and one step closer to doing the shopping herself.

61.
Be pushier

Start inviting the bereaved along on the errands you run on his behalf. Tell him he can sit in the car while you do the actual errand or come in with you and do it together. Plan the trip around lunch or dinner and slide into a restaurant to eat. Again, don't take no for an answer. "We have to eat lunch anyway," you might say. "Why not here?" Of course, remember our lesson in body language. If your neighbor turns away and starts walking home, it might be better to pick him up in the car and take him home. A little gentleness goes a long way. If you make him believe he's doing you a favor by having lunch with you, you might get him into that restaurant!

62.

Have his children over to your house

Neighborhoods come complete with children. The kids on your street might play together at every house in the neighborhood. If your bereaved neighbor has kids who've played at your house and are comfortable there, invite them over a little more often now. Academy Award–winning recovery behavior is especially prevalent when children are involved. The kids are grieving, too, but more capable of getting away from the grief for a couple of hours of play. Their parents may be trying to keep up appearances for the kids. This gets tiring for parents and children. If the neighborhood kids played at your house some of the time, keep it up, and make sure the bereaved's children are included.

63.

Take them along!

Heading to the beach? The movies? A science museum with a great exhibit on dinosaurs? Or just out trolling for something to do in the minivan? Invite your bereaved neighbors along. What's a few more kids and a couple of adults? Your presence can take the pressure off the parents to be perfect for their children. A day out and about with a few fun things to do can help your neighbors take a baby step toward their new life. Don't hesitate if the bereaved lost one of their children. This is every parent's worst nightmare, and your neighbors may be isolating themselves, not because they can't handle a day out, but because everyone else is keeping their distance. Up until now, maybe you were among those too terrified to arrange a family playdate. Remember, this isn't the wake or the funeral. This is play! Resolve to have fun. Treat your bereaved neighbors as you did in the past, which might have included trips like this. No matter how difficult it is for you, act normally.

It's possible that the parents may not be up to a family get-together. Ask whether it's OK to take the kids with your family. The kids could indulge in a little fun, and the parents could get some much-needed alone time. Even if it's only part of the family that joins yours for the day, it's still a big step along the path to healing for everyone.

64.
Help out with holidays and events

The first year after a loss is a long string of firsts that accentuate the loss. The first birthday without him. The first Easter, Memorial Day, or Thanksgiving without her. The first Christmas without that loved one at the table. Halloween (particularly that first one) has always been the hardest holiday for me. Nathan and I made a big deal out of Halloween, and I still miss making him a costume. My sister also loves Halloween, and on the first

Halloween after losing her nephew, while handing out candy at her door, a child dressed as a cow arrived at her house. Because I'd made Nathan a cow costume one year, my sister broke down.

It's not just the big events either. I miss my parents the most on my birthday and on their birthdays. My son was active in the 4-H club and participated in fairs to show the family dairy cows. When fair season comes around, I feel it. He sang in a choir; I still tear up when a children's choir performs. The first time at the first tee without a golfing buddy will be sad. When something good or interesting happens during the day and the bereaved can't share it with that loved one, it hurts.

So let's handle the hardest one first: the winter holidays. I'm going to talk about Christmas because that's my experience. No, you won't have to "do" your friend's entire Christmas. Even keeping with the assumption that the loss your neighbors suffered was a child, bereaved parents will make the effort to prepare as normal a family Christmas, Thanksgiving, or Easter as is possible. My son was an only child, but I've spoken with many bereaved parents who made the gigantic effort to keep family traditions intact for the sake of their other children. You can help with this.

Offer to shop with your bereaved neighbor. Remember, a grief shared is a sorrow halved. Having company on a holiday or birthday shopping trip is invaluable. Going with someone with a clearer head to make gift-buying decisions is priceless. And, let's face it, you'll get some of your own shopping done as well. While I know that Internet shopping is all the rage, if a grieving person shops alone online, it's a sad, solitary affair. Offering to go along on a shopping trip also gets your neighbor out of the house. It's practice for the future. Offer to help wrap, too.

At Christmas and birthdays there's a ton of planning and decorating to do. Offer to help with this as well. Don't make it obvious or make it look like a chore. My best advice is to offer to have a small Christmas party at their house with just your family and theirs. At the party, help put up the tree and decorate the house the way they always did. It'll be easier for them with someone else they know and love there to help. Offer to help plan their other child's birthday party. Help address invitations, clean the house, order the birthday cake, or arrange for a party at a local restaurant or business. Whatever you offer to do, make sure you discuss it with the parents completely to find out what their wishes are. Don't do something the parents don't want done, just so you can feel you helped. Holidays, birthdays, anniversaries, and so on, are really the province of the parents, not you. You can offer to help, but don't force them to do something they're not ready to do.

You can also help with other events. I read about a bereaved woman whose child was invited to a school friend's birthday party. She was too distraught and forgot the invitation. Her neighbor bought a birthday present and a card. She picked up her neighbor's child and took him to the party. Sometimes grieving parents are so overcome with the pain that they simply can't get their act together for the smaller events. And yet the child wants to go. This is where you can step in and help out.

So keep an eye on the calendar and the schedule of events, holidays, and birthdays. Try to remember what your grieving neighbor did in the past to celebrate or commemorate those occasions and offer to help.

65.
Shut up and listen to children

All of the previous invite-'em-along tips do come with some pitfalls. You, or more likely your children, may be cast in the role of confidant. Don't let this sneak up and grab you by the heart. Be prepared. At some point immediately after the loss (before or after the wake or funeral you took your child to), share with your child some of the concepts in this book. Don't make the mistake of keeping the loss a secret. Children can handle more than we think they can. In fact, for some adults, it's their own insecurities about death that stop them from talking to their children about a loss when it happens.

I'd advise that the most important concept to share with children is that they shouldn't treat their friend any differently than they did before. Odds are they wouldn't anyway. Naturally resilient, your children may scale the mountain of grief more quickly than you do. Naturally curious, they may find a way to work it out themselves early in the renewed relationship, with a few questions to the bereaved child. For the first few visits, until all the kids get their friendship back in balance, stay close by. Children aren't therapists, and no matter how much you prepare them, they may not know the right thing to do. If someone is in tears, step in and offer help.

Listening to bereaved children may give you information on their emotional well-being, feelings, and problems that they're not showing or telling their parents about. Academy Award–winning recoveries aren't the sole province of adults. After tragedy strikes, some things are expressed more easily to someone outside the family. You don't have to be a therapist. Just listen. If a bereaved child is exhibiting extreme behavior, tell his or her parents what you've learned. If something comes out in your conversation with a child, take the news to the parents immediately so they can take action to help.

A talk with the bereaved child's parents is a good thing to have before you start including the child in your family's activities. Assure the parents that you're listening to their child, bringing the information to them, and not acting on your own. Knowing the parents' wishes gives you welcome guidelines for helping the child. Talk with their parents ahead of time about how much the child knows. Take these steps to educate yourself, and then educate your kids so they can help, too.

66.
Recommend a children's grief support program

Do children grieve? Absolutely. Do adults always know what to look for or how to recognize the grief? Not always.

Linda Kelly, program director at the Center for Grieving Children in Portland, Maine, says, "People need to understand that children do grieve, and they grieve deeply." When asked how a parent or concerned adult can identify grief, she replied, "I think sometimes parents don't believe that children grieve because it is different from the way adults grieve. It's different in that it's episodic, so it looks very brief and intense, and it can change quickly to laughter or play. Often, children, especially younger children, do their work through play. It can be helpful just to sit with children while they're doing that work, and reflect back to them what you're seeing. It's important not to interpret what they're doing."

The Center for Grieving Children, like several others around the country, focuses on ways to offer peer support to bereaved children from the ages of three to eighteen. "Our groups are facilitated by well-qualified, well-trained volunteers. We provide a safe place, a safe container, so that the children and teens can open up, and we can explore their feelings about what has happened to them."

Mary Keane, the former executive director and founder of Mary's Place, a grieving center for children in Windsor,

Connecticut, points out that children's grief may resurface over a period of years, as they move from one developmental stage to another. She offered as an example a girl who came to Mary's Place at age four, after the death of a parent, and received support from the center for six years. "She wasn't the same little girl when she left as she was when she arrived," says Keane. "As she grew up, her grief manifested differently at each stage."

Such centers and dozens of others accept referrals in a number of ways. Most are charitable or nonprofit organizations and do not charge for the assistance they provide. Family members and friends, psychologists, physicians, clergy, hospital staff, funeral homes, and teachers are just a few of the people who may refer children for assistance. If you need to find such a center and don't know whom to ask for help, a simple Internet search for "grieving children" together with the name of your city will no doubt yield several results.

What about children and teens who need more help than the grief centers can provide? Linda Kelly says, "There are some worrisome behaviors, like dangerous risk-taking—climbing too high, running out into the road, threatening to hurt themselves or others, totally withdrawing from people—and for those children, we provide referrals to counselors who can help them." She added, "Any huge change in personality or how a child functions over a long period of time would be a good indication that the child needs some extra support."

Should children be involved in the funeral activities or in

family discussions about dead or dying relatives and friends? According to Kelly, it's best to make the decisions on a child-by-child basis. "We remind parents [that] they know their children better than we do. They should take the lead from the child. Explain, in an age-appropriate way, what to expect. Tell them what a wake looks like, what a funeral looks like, and how they will participate if they attend, and then let them decide."

Keane and Kelly both agree on one basic point. Bereaved children need to trust that what they're being told is true. Says Kelly, "We always say, tell the children the truth—even young children. It needs to be age appropriate, but most often, children already know more about the death than adults think. So, to establish trust with the children, it's important to be as truthful as you can about what has happened."

If all of the above fail and your neighbor's child exhibits extreme grief behavior, suggest a children's grief support program to the parents.

6

WHEN THE BEREAVED IS YOUR BEST FRIEND OR A MEMBER OF YOUR FAMILY

Of all the relationships we've discussed so far, your relationship with your best friend or family member who is grieving is the most intimate and therefore offers you the most opportunities to help and support. You know your friend or relative better than any of the other people who've offered to help. You've shared ups and downs before. Now you get to help again. You, as a person closer to the bereaved, will get the most satisfaction out of being needed and helping ease the pain of grief. Of course, more is expected of you as well. But I know that horrible feeling of not being able to fix something. You've probably wished, more than once, that it was happening to you instead of to your best friend or family member. Grief is difficult, but I also know how hard it is to watch people in pain and know that you can't do anything to take it away. The more challenging but rewarding tips for helping the bereaved are left to you.

67.

Smarten up! Learn about the process of grief

Whatever that is! The grieving process, once thought to have been cast in stone by Elisabeth Kübler-Ross's book *On Death and Dying*, vies for position among numerous differing opinions. The resultant controversy and volume of output make it difficult to know what's up.

Thankfully, you have me! Yep, I'll turn the muddy swamp to a clear mountain lake. I figure living through it gives me as much credibility as any therapist or psychologist. So there!

Let's start at almost the beginning. The stages of grief adopted from Kübler-Ross's work are the following:

1. Denial
2. Anger
3. Bargaining
4. Depression
5. Acceptance

This model is the result of Kübler-Ross's studies of her patients' emotional responses to news of their impending deaths. Along with embracing and utilizing, to great benefit, the stages in the process of accepting death, the world made a leap and adopted the same stages for the process of mourning.

As it turns out, even Kübler-Ross admitted that the two events were different and that the five stages of dying would not describe the experience of those in mourning. That said, let's look at denial. I have to admit that the denial stage caused me some confusion. I didn't experience denial when my son died. It was all too real for me. And it didn't seem possible to me that anyone going through all the rigmarole of a wake, funeral, and burial could possibly be in denial over the death of a loved one. Turns out I was right.

Writing for the Grief Recovery Institute website, Russell Friedman and John W. James made their case in the article "Are There Actual Stages of Grieving?": "In all of our years of experience, working with tens of thousands of grievers, we have rarely met anyone 'in denial' that a loss has occurred," wrote Friedman and James. "They say, 'Since my mom died, I have had a hard time.' There is no denial in that comment. There is a very clear acknowledgement that there has been a death."

That has also been my experience. I've never talked with anyone in denial about a death.

Anger is another of Kübler-Ross's stages for grief that bites the dust for those of us grieving the death of a loved one. Anger after the death of a loved one commonly stems from unresolved issues raised during the living relationship. Those who are aware of the importance of talking about and settling old issues or of bringing closure to rifts in a relationship make sure that old hurts are forgiven, misunderstandings are cleared up, and old differences resolved before their loved ones die. If love and understanding flow through the relationship between the dying and the bereaved, after-death anger can often be avoided.

However, dealing with anger can't be regulated any more than dealing with grief. As in my case, anger may lie submerged and unrecognized for weeks, months, and even years, simply because there seems to be no reason for it—except to rail against fate. Anger may come to others who couldn't say their final good-byes. So, while anger can be a part of the grieving process for some, it isn't for everyone.

So how about bargaining? In the dying process, bargaining consists of terminal patients making deals with a supreme being to postpone or avoid death altogether. Well, it's a little late for the bargaining stage for the bereaved, isn't it? I mean, their loved ones are already dead. What is there to bargain for? Again this is a stage that just doesn't fit the mourning process.

Ah, but stage four, depression, now that one unfortunately fits, doesn't it? As does the final stage, acceptance.

Another problem, according to the experts, is the use of the word *stages* itself. *Stages* implies, actually imposes, that grieving is a neat process with measurable steps that begin and end on cue and move the griever, conveyor-like, on to the next stage. Mourners have come to believe that they can pass through and finish a stage before going on to the next. The stages give mourners the illusion that they will experience each one once, move on to the next, and then reach the finish line—whole, complete, and back to normal. But grieving is not linear, and there is no definite time line for the process.

In reality, there's no assurance that, just because your friend dealt with depression once, he's finished with it. Mourning is a roller-coaster ride with lots of loops. He's up, he's down, he's numb, depressed, yearning, depressed again, and then—damn!—numb again. That's the ride that your friend is on. There is no neat beginning and ending.

So, because the stages of dying don't apply to grief, and because there are problems with the word *stages*, some folks at the forefront of grief research switched to using the word *phases*. Unfortunately phase theorists have yet to get their act together regarding the number of phases there are in the mourning process. Theories range from three phases to twelve! Yikes!

Because I am neither scientist nor psychiatrist, but active participant in the mourning process, here I have selected what I think is the most relevant and useful model of grief. After wading waist-high in papers on phases, stages, steps, segments, and more, I'm actually going to select an old theory of grief behavior. According to a 2007 article at the *Forbes* site HealthDay News, the oldest theory of mourning goes like this:

1. Shock-numbness
2. Yearning-searching
3. Disorganization-despair
4. Reorganization

Although the titles are from HealthDay News, the explanations of each that follow are strictly my own and are based on my active, ongoing participation in the process of grief.

1. **Shock-numbness.** This one is right on. Whether everyone knew in advance that a loved one was terminal or if the death was sudden and came as a surprise, we are never ready for death. We knew my son was terminal, but when he died, I slipped easily into numbness. In this phase, your friend will not be able to make decisions as simple as what to wear, what to eat, or when to go to bed. Guide her gently. Shock-numbness flows into, overlaps, and coexists with the next phase.

2. **Yearning-searching.** The yearning part of this portion of grief can manifest when the bereaved glimpses someone who looks just like the loved one who died. When he realizes it's a doppelgänger, the bereaved can be catapulted back to shock and numbness.

   I remember one incident when my sister and I were driving to the mall to do a little shopping. We passed a young man mowing his front yard. We saw him only from the back, but my sister looked at me, her eyes wide, and I looked at her. We had both thought it was Nathan. It was extremely upsetting and unnerving. The remainder of the trip was subdued.

   The yearning also results from the giant hole left behind, the loneliness of missing a loved one. The bereaved wonders how he will ever fill that hole, how he will ever go on alone.

   My searching was my guilt trip. I reviewed everything I'd done in directing my son's care and found, I believed, many mistakes I'd made that unnecessarily shortened his life. I went on a wild-goose chase of "What if I'd…" "What if I hadn't…" "I should have found another doctor, another hospital, another treatment, one more test." "If only…" "If only…" If only…"

If you see these signs of guilt and searching in your grieving friend, arrange for a phone call from the doctor to go over the treatment again to reassure your friend that everything possible was done. Just a note: guilt isn't easily cured. Guilt will come back. Be prepared to reassure your friend many times that his actions, or lack thereof, did not cause his loved one's death.

Yearning-searching with shock-numbness close behind will inevitably flow into, overlap, and coexist with the next phase.

3. **Disorganization-despair.** This is what happens when the yearning and searching have proven fruitless. I can remember letting mail and laundry pile up and the fridge run empty. Going to the grocery store when what I needed to do was get gas in the car. I spent a lot of time in the apartment, not getting out of my pajamas. I couldn't. I still hadn't done the laundry! People came and picked up things I thought Nathan would want them to have. I'd cry when they left. When all that was left was stuff I couldn't bear to part with, I shut the door to his bedroom. I cried a lot then but was surprised to find that part of that gaping hole had filled. Although they took symbols of Nathan away with them, they left a memory, an anecdote, some tears and love that tumbled into the hole and made it smaller—not a lot smaller but smaller nonetheless.

The despair component of mourning can become the most

dangerous. An article published at the Mayo Clinic website (www.mayoclinic.com) estimated that anywhere from 6 percent to 20 percent of bereaved people may experience a condition called complicated grief. While the research on complicated grief is sparse, it appears most often in those bereaved who suffer a sudden, untimely, or violent loss. Indications of complicated grief are the much-magnified indications of normal grief: shock, numbness, yearning, searching, disorganization, and despair. You'll know if your friend has complicated grief. You won't be able to miss it. If you have an iota of doubt that your friend is experiencing complicated grief, then he or she probably isn't. Complicated grief is as obvious as the sunrise each day.

Disorganization-despair, yearning-searching, and shock-numbness will flow into, overlap, and coexist with the next phase.

4. Reorganization. This phase continues until our own death. We gradually add filler to that gaping hole that was our loved one's place in our lives each time we take over, or we find someone else to take over, a task that our lost loved one had fulfilled. New interests, new friends, every laugh, every enjoyed social event, and every old interest renewed add filler to the hole. Soon new pathways build around the hole. It doesn't ever go away, but your friend or relative develops coping mechanisms so he or she falls into it less and less.

How long does mourning last? Only your god knows for sure. Oh, there are averages out there, some of them based on solid research and some of them just guesses. Again from my nonscientific and nonpsychiatric but active participant perch, I pronounce that there is no time limit. Don't impose one on your friend. Let him take all the time he needs, be it days, weeks, months, or years.

68.
Give her permission to grieve

Huh? Well, allowing a person to actively grieve wherever, whenever, and however they need to is like the city officials announcing you need a new dump. Everybody is for it as long as it's not built anywhere near them. Society's—our—inability to handle tears or, for God's sake, to actually talk about loss signals the bereaved to adopt the Academy Award–winning recovery role.

"Tears? Don't be silly! Just my allergies kicking in."

"Oh, I'm doing fine! Almost back to normal. Thanks for asking. Been golfing lately?"

Most bereaved people are too afraid that they'll offend or upset someone to fully participate in the grief process. For them, mourning must be controlled, confined, and compartmentalized behind the closed doors of their empty homes.

While mourning alone has become the norm, it certainly isn't healthy. The bereaved need a shoulder to cry on even if he won't admit it. He needs someone to listen to him and share stories. He needs someone to be quiet with and someone to stick with him at those first awkward social events.

Mostly he needs someone to tell him over and over again that mourning isn't just OK; it's vital. Someone who says, "There, there, that's it. Just cry it all out." Someone who asks about memories of the deceased and actually listens to them.

Be the one to give your friend the time, space, companionship, and permission to grieve. You'll both feel better!

69.
Validate his feelings

Feelings, unlike stages or phases of grief, run the gamut from numbness to hypersensitivity, from rage to acceptance, from loneliness to fear, from insecurity to confidence, from wanting to be left alone to being afraid to be left alone. And all of them, and the myriad other feelings that mourners experience, are OK.

You may find it hard to get your friend or family member to open up and talk about his feelings. After all, he's also been socialized to keep mourning a deep, dark secret never to be shown the light of day. Well, here's a method I know works.

My best friend and sister of my heart, Kathy, called me daily.

"Just wanted to check in," she'd say when I answered the phone. "How was your day?" Well, to be honest, my day had been pretty crappy, but I didn't want to tell her that. Why ruin her day?

"Oh, OK," I'd answer. "The ladies at work took me to lunch."

"That's great!" Kathy said. "Did you have a good time? Why'd they take you out?"

"Well, they said they wanted to be sure I knew they knew how I felt and that if I needed anything to just ask."

There was the slightest pause.

"And how did that make you feel?" she asked, and didn't say another word.

As the silence lengthened, my reserve cracked, and I just had to fill that silence.

"Well, I know they're trying to help, but they *don't* know how I feel." And I was off and running like a babbling brook.

The key to success with Kathy's method is to remember that, as human beings, we hate silence! And the longer it lasts, the more antsy we get until we just can't stand it anymore and we start talking. I don't know how many times Kathy used that technique on me, but it worked every time.

Finally, when talking to the bereaved, don't tell him you know how he feels. You don't. Grief is as individual as DNA, and your experience will never match that of another person. Here's what to say instead: "I can only imagine how you feel, but I know that whatever you're feeling is the right thing for you. Never let anyone tell you to feel any differently than you do."

Just so you don't forget it, write that on the blackboard a hundred times!

70.
Validate grief

We all accept that it is appropriate to grieve for a loved one at the funeral. And, yeah, OK, you can be sad for a week or two—or, hey, maybe even a month. But several months? A year? Isn't it time to, like, move on? Get over it?

As I mentioned in Tip #47, while that would be more convenient and comfortable for the rest of us, the truth is that grief knows no time. So many factors come into play—and only the bereaved knows how tightly entwined her life was with that of the departed, how big a hole it will leave in her life.

If we have other loved ones in our lives to support us through the grieving process, and if we have interests and work to distract us, then, perhaps, we move through the grieving process a little more quickly.

Sometimes we don't. Sometimes it takes years—and years. In fact, for most of us, the wound heals but leaves a scar that, with very little effort, can open and bleed again, especially around the time of the anniversary of the birth or death of the loved one. An article by the International Critical Incident Stress Foundation (www.icisf.org) says, "For some, the anniversary date is a powerful reminder of loss." Family members are reminded of the gaping hole left by the death of the loved one. The article also says that, for those who may have tried to deny the experience of grief, the anniversary "may break through their defenses and produce unexpected grief and feelings of despair."

We are never who we were before the death of a loved one. So don't ask someone who is grieving to just get on with life. Don't tell her to get over it. Instead, listen to what she has to say about her grief—how it keeps her up at night, how sad she feels every Saturday morning when the weekly phone call from her mother doesn't come, or how she "just misses her so much!"

You may have heard it all before—maybe just yesterday—but she obviously needs to say it again, and as a good friend, you need to listen again, to put an arm around your friend and say, "Of course you feel that way. I know how much you loved her."

Then try some of the previous tips, like planning an activity, watching a movie together, and so forth. Honor her grief and the time she needs to heal from it.

71.
Validate relief

Validating relief can be a little tricky. In the midst of our pain and sorrow over the death of someone we love, there may also be a measure of relief if the person was ill or old or anything else that made the past few years, months, or days one challenge after another, even if none of us want to admit that.

Even more difficult to understand for many of us is that sometimes the death is a relief because it is a release from a difficult relationship, whether with a spouse, a parent, or a sibling. We know we are not supposed to speak ill of the dead, so with that secret sense of relief may come a measure of shame or guilt: *How could I think that? I must be a terrible person!* Well, you're probably not. Just an imperfect human one.

The end of the stress and trauma of a difficult relationship, which can entail anything from a seemingly unending schedule of caring for a sick and dying loved one, to mental illness or addiction, to verbal, emotional, or physical violence, can leave the bereaved confused, sad, and—yes—relieved. In the midst of that emotional morass, the last thing we need, even though it is not uncommon, is guilt—or more guilt.

Instead, give the bereaved space to accept what he is feeling by mentioning how tired he must be or how hard the past few days must have been. Or the bereaved may confide in you about his relief. Just listen, and then say, "After everything you've been through, I can imagine why you feel that way."

Remember that it is never helpful to the bereaved to force our ideas of acceptable grieving on him.

72.
Spend time with her in her home

Don't ask her out to a movie. Rent one, and go to her house to watch it. (Bring a pizza along, too—by now she's probably sick and tired of all the healthy food this book advocates!) Yes,

I know in Tip #25 I suggested taking the bereaved out for a movie. But you, as a best friend or family member, have a closer relationship with the bereaved. She is likely to be more comfortable having you in her home, especially in the early period of grief when she may not want to go out. Going out means putting on a fake happy face for all those strangers. Trying not to show grief in public is exhausting. What your friend or family member needs is company—someone who doesn't care if she's sad, if she cries once in a while, if she just wants to sit and do nothing. Someone who will be there so she's not doing all those grief things alone all the time. My best friend called me every night, and it was always my choice to talk about my son's death and how I was grieving, or to just compare notes on the day. Kathy didn't care what I blathered on about; she listened. She didn't judge me either. She didn't tell me to move on with life, that enough time had passed, and that I shouldn't be grieving anymore. She visited me at my house and somehow knew when I was up for a trip out into the world to a gem or quilt show. The best advice I can give you is that the best way to help the bereaved is to be like Kathy and just be there.

73.
Offer to help with funeral arrangements

What about the funeral? How does it happen? Who does the planning? Unless the deceased has taken care of everything in advance, something that takes immediate priority upon a death is arranging for the funeral. At a time when emotions are running high and perhaps not everyone who needs to be involved lives locally, you can use your skills and time to make the job of planning the funeral activities easier for the bereaved.

Make calls to area funeral homes to discuss the types of services they offer and roughly how much to expect to pay for them. John C. Carmon, the former president of the National Association of Funeral Directors and owner of Carmon Family Funeral Homes in Connecticut, says, "There is no funeral home I know of anywhere that charges anything for sitting down with a family or talking to them to discuss their options and choices." In fact, many funeral homes now post pricing information on their websites so you can get some idea of what funeral services and merchandise such as caskets, outer containers, burial urns, and so forth, will cost. Most funeral homes offer affordable options and ways for families to pay if money is tight.

Ask the bereaved whether his loved one had any special wishes for the funeral service—sometimes these things are discussed in family conversations and then forgotten during the stress of the days after a death occurs. The gentle question, "Was there anything in particular she wanted?" might lead to useful information in planning the service. Don't forget to ask the bereaved if there is anything special he wants for the service, too. If the funeral is military, there will be conversations with local units to arrange the honor guard and flag presentation.

Most funeral directors are more than willing to accommodate requests for special or unique activities, within reason, as part of the service. Carmon says, "We're human. So much of what happens surrounding a death involves our hearts, our emotions, our feelings, and they need to be dealt with." He added, "What's most important is the funeral service, the celebration of life, the things they do to interconnect with their family and friends, things that they find to be extremely meaningful are really all part of planning that special service—memorial service, funeral, gathering, whatever they call it. Whatever merchandise they need is really incidental to that. It should be what they feel is appropriate, but the important thing is the service."

Sit in on the meetings with the clergy or spiritual adviser your friend has selected to lead the funeral service. Sometimes, just having a friend nearby will provide enough support to the bereaved that he can make good decisions about how he wants things handled.

Offer to be a private livery service—there may be people arriving from out of town who will need shuttling to and from the airports, train stations, funeral home, and cemetery. Find out who's coming from where and when they're arriving, and then go get them, and take them back again when it's time for them to leave.

If there is to be a gathering after the funeral for friends and family, you can offer to be the point person for getting the location ready, whether it's a restaurant or the bereaved's home. If it's at a restaurant, make sure that the owners know to keep the group together, possibly in a private dining room, how many people to expect, how long the event will last, and who will be responsible for paying the bill at the end. If it's at the bereaved's home, do the setup and cleanup so that he won't be left with a mess after everyone leaves. Make arrangements for refreshments to be available, and keep track of who's bringing what so that afterward thank-you notes can be sent.

Encourage the bereaved to focus on creating a service that commemorates the life of his loved one in a way that truly reflects the person he or she was and gives people an opportunity to express condolences and love to one another and to the family. When asked about the importance of ritual and ceremony, Carmon says, "They bring us structure, they bring us help, but they also bring people together so that they can support one another. If we don't have that mechanism—to bring people together, to care about one another—so that they can feel that, it's very difficult to heal."

74.
Do the eulogy

This is simpler than it sounds: just tell stories. But you do need to plan ahead. Here's how:

1. Imagine and then jot down the one great impression the deceased has left with you: she was mother to everyone she met, a good sport, the last one to leave a party.

2. Now make a list of some favorite stories that show that. The time that she stopped the car to rescue a terrified opossum from Route 44 or that he tried to roast a thirty-pound suckling pig one Christmas just because his mother had always wanted one—those stories tell us more about the person than all the oratory heaped on a Roman senator from the steps of the Forum.

3. If you don't know specific stories, ask your friend or family member. For the bereaved, retelling those memories to you can be surprisingly freeing.

4. Don't shy away from the funny stories. Chances are that by the time you rise to speak, there will have been plenty of talk about monumental loss and the celestial choir warming up in the wings. Now is the time to remind people that the memories are still alive and anxious to come out and help them heal.

5. As you make notes and think about how to word your stories, be specific. Instead of, "George lived a long life," try, "When asked what he attributed his long life to, George replied, 'The fact that I haven't died yet.'" We can almost see the twinkle in George's blue eyes as he said that.

6. Arrange the best of these stories (three is a good number) in some order. A friend of mine began her father's eulogy by saying the only possession of his she'd requested was his pitch pipe. First, she described the times she had heard him from her bedroom as a young child while he set the right

starting note for his barbershop quartet. Next, she told of the Christmas Eves when he, as a grandfather, led four generations in singing "The Twelve Days of Christmas." Finally, she drew the stories together by noting that her father used his pitch pipe—as he used the rest of his life—to draw people together, set the right tone, and encourage them to harmonize. She concluded by reading to her father's spirit the words of one of his favorite barbershop quartet songs: "Good-Bye, My Coney Island Baby." Her final words, "Good-bye, Daddy," left people smiling and crying at the same time.

7. Stand and deliver. Try not to read. Keep in mind what the mother of one nervous young woman told her before a presentation, "Just get up there and pretend you're as good as everybody else." You are.

8. When you are done, move quietly and slowly back to your seat. The pause will give people a chance to get ready for the next part of the ceremony.

75.
Create a testimonial

Something that's becoming more common at funeral and memorial services is the addition of a video presentation that focuses on and honors the life of the deceased. Video memorials depict the story of a person's life through a montage of photographs, music, audio, and video.

There are several reasons this is a good way to help the bereaved. First of all, viewing the video provides a much-needed, welcome chance for grieving people to share their memories and focus on the happy times in their loved one's lifetime. Second, the viewing can often change the atmosphere of the gathering, generating a sense of celebration and appreciation that can lift people's spirits. Finally, the video can be viewed many times, providing a way for bereaved people to reconnect with their loved ones.

If you can use presentation software, make a slide show for the services and surrounding activities. While bulletin boards of photos are lovely, a slide show allows more people easier access to the photos. You can rent a computer projector and a screen for use before and after the service; churches and community organizations often have their own equipment and will allow you to use it. An easily copied CD of the slide show will also be a much appreciated memento for family and friends. Most people familiar with computers and with access to digital photos of the person can make a simple presentation. Decide on the organization of the photos: chronological; thematic; job, hobby, and travel sections; or a combination (chronology within a hobby, for example). Use whatever seems to fit the person's life.

Most people today take photos on digital cameras, so they are already in the format you need. Photos more than a few years old will probably have to be scanned and digitized for this use—use the highest resolution for scanning that you can because they'll be blown up so much on the big screen. If you know a death is impending, and the family wants and will appreciate a video presentation, start scanning as soon as possible and prudent. Ask the family which photos are most important to include, and digitize those first. If you have access to a scanner, great, but if you don't, take the photos to a local copy center to scan them, and get a CD you can use to transfer the images to your computer. Once the photos and any music you want to use are on your hard drive, you'll use the presentation software to create your project. Include photos of the deceased with family and friends.

Action photos and photos of common activities are often more interesting than posed photos. Posed photos tend to be more flattering. Try for a combination.

The photos won't always fit the shape of the slide screen, so a background color or pattern will be needed. Use a black background for black and white photos. For color photo backgrounds, choose a color that will make the featured person "pop"—the color of her blouse, for example. For a background for the opening name and dates, you might choose the garden he created or the quilt she made for her granddaughter. Make the name and dates large enough and dark enough to be clearly seen. Use a font that is plain enough to read quickly: a slide show presented in a sanctuary or gathering hall will not show up as well as it does on the computer screen.

Music is a nice touch, particularly music meaningful to the deceased or the family and friends. It can be inserted into the presentation from a CD, the Web, or another source, and can be assigned to loop or to play for a specific number of slides.

If you have some technical skills and video-editing software, you can also create a video memorial that includes movies and more features than are available in a slideshow presentation. However, if you don't have the technical expertise or the time to do it yourself, you can hire professional videographers to create the video for you. You provide the videographer with the materials, and he or she delivers the finished product for you for an agreed-upon fee. Fees for professional video memorials depend on the length of the video and how many photos, captions, effects (dissolves and fades), video and audio clips, and musical pieces are included. Most videographers also provide custom artwork for the media they produce. Expect to pay half the fee up-front and the remainder upon delivery of the finished product.

There are some challenges that you should watch for, according to Marsha Browne, a partner at Keepsake Digital Services (KDS Productions), in Massachusetts. How do you know whether the videographer is any good? Browne says you should ask to see some samples of previous work. "You can get a pretty good idea of what your memorial video will be like [by] watching a few samples. Does the videographer have a good sense of composition and pacing? Do the transitions between images and audio feel natural, and is the video telling a moving and coherent story? A good videographer pays attention to these things."

Don't forget to factor in the time required to deliver materials. This is especially true if you are working remotely with a videographer. While some carriers guarantee overnight delivery, you have to pay extra to guarantee arrival by a certain hour, which can drive up your costs dramatically.

Always indicate where the subject of the memorial is in each image. Browne says, "There's nothing worse than when the image zooms in on a sister, brother, or best friend instead of the subject, because we don't know who the people are." Browne also asks, "How do you want people to feel after watching it? It's surprising how often the words *happy* and *comforted* come up as answers to that question."

Specify the format you want for the finished video—CD, DVD, VCD, or something else. Browne says, "Tell me where you intend to show the video—will it be at somebody's house, using a home theater system that includes an LCD projector and a screen, on a computer screen in the lobby of the funeral home or at a restaurant or church, or is it for sending it to friends and family who cannot attend the funeral in person? Are you planning to post it on the Internet? Will the video be played in Europe, Asia, or Australia? Let the videographer know because of the differences in playback technology." A few videographers will even go the extra step of providing you with the equipment necessary to screen the video for a nominal charge.

Is it better to use a local small service or a big franchised one? While Browne acknowledges that there are savings with bigger outfits who deal in high volumes, there are advantages to working with smaller companies. "For one thing, the small company will be more willing to personalize your memorial—many of the larger ones use standard templates from their library, whether or not it's suited to your loved one. You don't want to end up with a cookie-cutter version."

Talk to the videographer about the person who's being memorialized. There should be a match between the video's pacing and story, and the person whose life is being depicted. "Our goal is to portray the subject in a way that honors his or her life. We recently made a memorial video about a popular woman who was a positive influence on a number of people. The video was played in a large auditorium at a professional conference, and was seen by both people who knew and loved her, and people who'd never met her. Our goal was to make every person who didn't know her wish they had, and every person who did know her remember why they cared about her."

Keep the slide show to ten or fifteen minutes so people can see it all. Four or five seconds is generally enough for each image. With this time frame, those who are watching can often see it two or three times during the gatherings. The video memorial will be a beautiful keepsake that can help family and friends in the grieving process. Browne says, "One client who lives out of state, and with whom we worked remotely, wrote to me weeks after her husband's memorial service. She said that she now watches the video almost daily, and it makes her feel comforted and close to him."

76.
Create a website

If you are comfortable using computers and the Internet, something you can do to help the bereaved to honor his loved one is to create a memorial website or blog. The website will be a place online where people can go to share their thoughts and memories about the deceased and to offer condolences to the family. This is especially helpful to grieving family and friends who are scattered geographically. Ideally, you will be able to create, publish, and register the website within a day or so of the loved one's death. Ask the family if it's OK to create the website, and explain the benefit to them. If they're not interested, don't push.

There are whole books written about creating websites and blogs, but, really, it doesn't have to be complicated or time consuming. There are free tools available that make the job simple and fast. One of the best, most user-friendly ones around is Google's Blogger utility. The process is very straightforward.

First, register for a free account at www.blogger.com. Blogger's offering includes free hosting, which means you don't have to register a domain name, and the site provides disk space on the Blogger servers for users to store their images.

Then select a URL that will be easy for people to remember (such as http://jerrysmith.blogspot.com, or http://janefrancis doe.blogspot.com). At the same time, create a meaningful title for the blog ("We Won't Forget Jerry," "Our Beloved Jane," or even "In Memoriam").

Add meta tags to the blog header—these tags will assist viewers in finding your memorial website, even if they've forgotten the URL. Use the loved one's full name, nickname, family name, and even addresses as meta tags. This way, if anybody types one or more of the meta tags into a search engine, he or she is likely to reach the blog.

Next, pick a template from among the dozens offered. Just remember that, for memorial blogs, simpler designs are often most effective, and besides, the purpose is not to show off your ability to sling HTML or dazzle viewers with every bell and whistle imaginable. The template you choose should allow people to enter comments in response to your entries. It's up to you to decide whether you will permit unmoderated comments. When comments are moderated, they first go into a queue awaiting your approval before they are published to the site. With Blogger, as the owner of the blog you always have the option of deleting unwanted or unwelcome entries, even if they are unmoderated.

Use the supplied WYSIWYG ("what you see is what you get") editor to type in the first entry, which is typically a few paragraphs that provide visitors to the website with information about the deceased, any personal notes you want to add, and a photograph or two.

Once you're satisfied with the results in Preview mode, click Publish, and the blog is immediately available for viewing by anyone. Send an email to family and friends that provides a link to the blog, and encourage them to visit it and post their comments. If people want to contribute photographs, terrific—tell them to send you the photos via email, and then you can go back into the Blogger editor, add them, and republish the blog.

You can also add a free site meter to the blog that lets you know how much Internet traffic (or hits) the site is getting, and you can set your blog preferences so that you receive an email notification every time somebody posts a comment. There's no time limit for how long a blog can stay up; once published, the blog will stay active until you delete it.

Your bereaved friends will appreciate your effort on their behalf.

77.
Know when to hold 'em, and know when to hug 'em

Unless you've been living in a cave, you've seen stories about people who volunteer their time to sit in hospital nurseries and rock babies. You may have also seen stories about the stunted physical, emotional, and intellectual growth of children in orphanages when they've been deprived of nurturing touch. The need for touch doesn't disappear with age. It's important for people who are ill, and particularly for those who are grieving. Think I'm kidding?

Dr. Charmaine Griffiths, spokesperson for the British Heart Foundation, a registered charity that invests in pioneering research, support, and care for heart patients, said, "Scientists are increasingly interested in the possibility that positive emotions can be good for your health. This study [which was conducted at the University of North Carolina–Chapel Hill and looked at the effects of touch, especially holding hands and hugging, on stress response levels] has reinforced research findings that support from a partner, in this case a hug from a loved one, can have beneficial effects on heart health." Hugging says a lot without words.

We all know that depression is a real problem for the bereaved. Tiffany Field, PhD, director of the Touch Research Institute (University of Miami Medical School), formally established the first center in the world devoted solely to the study of touch and its application in science and medicine. The institute's studies have shown that touch in the form of massage therapy reduces pain and stress hormones, and alleviates symptoms of depression. So I ask you, is it so big a leap to imagine the power of a gentle embrace, a held hand, a kiss on the cheek?

Two guidelines to remember: Ask first, with a sincere and questioning look. Be compassionate, not passionate (you know what I mean).

So come on. Hugging requires no special training, equipment, license, or fee. You want to help someone who is grieving? Open your arms.

78.
Help with the pets

Even though they are usually considered part of the family, pets of the bereaved or of the family of the bereaved can easily be forgotten in the attempt to deal with all the human grief. But animals still need to be fed and watered, exercised, and groomed.

They also need love and affection because pets grieve, too, and their grieving period can last anywhere from several weeks to six or more months.

Cats and dogs, especially, are sensitive not just to the loss of a beloved companion but also to the grief and sadness of those around them. In response to grief, cats and dogs will sometimes pace, vocalize, refuse to eat, or constantly go to the door or a window to wait for the return of the loved one. Some animals become so depressed that their lives are threatened.

So do both the bereaved and her animal companion a big favor by offering to not only do the twice-daily walks and the feeding but also to sit with the animal, petting it and talking to it. Offer to make a trip with the animal to the vet if it is due for shots or a checkup, or if in its grief it seems unwell.

Just like humans, in their times of grief, pets need more love and affection.

79.
Offer to help with the paperwork

There is no way around it. A death creates enough paperwork to make a good bonfire. But as tempting as it might be to burn that pile of papers, envelopes, condolence cards, bills, and junk mail, or at the very least, ignore them for a couple of days or weeks…or months, the results would not be good.

When people die, there are steps that have to be taken to legally deal with property, taxes, banks, insurance companies, and governmental agencies. Grieving spouses and family members potentially face a mountain of paperwork at a time when they feel least capable of dealing with it. You can make their lives more bearable in the aftermath of a death if you offload some of the tasks onto yourself. Help your friends create a list of required actions they must take, and offer your assistance in completing the tasks.

- **Thank-you cards.** One of the first tasks that falls to bereaved people is writing thank-you cards to those who offered help and support to them before, during, and after their loved one's death. The number of cards varies with each situation, but they are always handwritten notes, and as such, they must also have handwritten envelopes. The thank-you cards go to anyone who acted as a pallbearer; the clergy; people who provided spiritual guidance during the funeral services;

friends who babysat, drove others in the funeral procession, provided food, or gave gifts; and those who made donations in the name of the deceased.

Offer to sit with your friend as he writes the notes, and then take part by filling out the names and addresses on the envelopes, then stamping, sealing, and taking them to the post office. If you can afford it, you might even want to buy the stamps, cards, and envelopes for your friend, so that he doesn't have to think about it.

If you do this, you score a plus on two counts: The task gets finished, and you spend time with your grieving friend or family member.

- **Death certificates, insurance companies, and government agencies.** For people to receive death benefits from Social Security and to transfer property legally, all the proper forms must be on file. The funeral director actually files the death certificate with the Bureau of Vital Statistics. Preview a sample of the completed death certificate with your friend before it's sent for certification with the Bureau of Vital Statistics. Pay attention to the details—especially the numbers. The wrong Social Security number, birth date, or death date will cause problems later. After the filing, offer to get several copies of the certificate for your friend from the local vital records office. The certificate is required to receive insurance claims, to close bank accounts, to transfer ownership of property and real estate, and to apply for Social Security and military benefits.

When my friend Marsha Browne's father died, two days after the funeral she discovered that he owned several insurance policies with three or four companies that named her mother as beneficiary. Marsha spent days sorting through the policies, calling the companies, and arranging for the claims to be transferred to her mother's bank account. The process was complicated by the fact that larger companies had acquired some of the issuing companies, so she had to find out how to get to the correct claims departments. She later said that her mother would have never been able to deal with the bureaucracy, given the depth of her grief. You can be sure that nobody from the insurance company was going to call her mother and offer to pay out a claim.

- **Probate court.** Depending on the size and value of the estate, filing in probate court may or may not be necessary. Different jurisdictions have different laws, so it's a good idea to check with a legal representative before you do anything. Offer to speak with a lawyer on the bereaved's behalf, and make any phone calls to banks and the court for answers to any questions the bereaved has. Unfortunately, you can sometimes end up in a catch-22. Banks will not allow access to personal safe-deposit boxes without certified copies of the probate filing. But what if the will is in the safe-deposit box? A lawyer who specializes in estate planning should be able to untangle the knot of requirements so that you can move forward. This back-and-forth is exactly the kind of thing a grief-stricken spouse or family member doesn't want to deal with, so your help in navigating the legal mazes will be invaluable to them.

- **Mail and bills.** While you can't really open another person's mail, you can certainly assist in organizing it so that when the bereaved person is ready to address bills, notes, and forms, she has an idea of what's waiting for her or requires action. On a clean workspace reserved for this purpose, separate the mail into piles: circulars and ads, personal notes, bills and notices, and claim forms. Label each pile, and use sticky notes on the envelopes to indicate which pieces need immediate attention. This is especially useful because it gives the bereaved some sense of control over what's coming at her.

    Also offer to take over paying the bills and reconciling the checkbook until the bereaved can cope with doing it. Many men and women have never done either, and instead used to rely on the deceased to handle the job for them. If that's the case, she probably doesn't know how to handle the monthly cash flow and could get into financial trouble without your help.

80.

Make sure she is as financially stable as possible

If you haven't figured it out by now, people who are grieving aren't always thinking clearly. Because I'm talking about the bereaved who is your best friend or a family member, chances are good that you know the bereaved's financial situation.

If she is financially secure, ask whether she needs help with insurance claim forms, change forms on bank accounts, investments, and so on. If you have financial expertise yourself, offer it. Remind her that something as simple as withdrawing retirement funds or cashing out a CD in one month as opposed to another can trigger penalties or an unwanted tax event. If you don't have such expertise, or if financial intimacy makes either of you uncomfortable, get the name of a good financial planner. Offer to set up an appointment. Offer to accompany her and take notes.

One of my own friends has worked for decades with financial adviser Robert W. Gillikin, CLU. When her father died and she received an inheritance, he cautioned her by saying that most baby boomers deplete their inheritances in three years or less. Why? Because they spend the money foolishly. Why? Because grief can so easily cloud their judgment.

Sometimes when the bereaved has lost a spouse, she succumbs to the impulse to get rid of things they shared—not just the bed, but the car, the house. She can just as easily feel compelled to fill the emptiness with a new bed, a new car, a new house, a new life. When my friend Zita's mother died, her father tore up all the flower gardens, one of the joys they shared together.

As Gillikin put it, "I tell people who are grieving to take care of the basics. Don't let the mortgage payments fall through the cracks. Keep the insurance, utilities, and credit cards paid. Let life settle. Grieving is painful but it's part of the healing process. Spending large sums of money when the mind is clouded doesn't shortcut grief and can actually be hazardous, especially financially."

So if the bereaved is your friend or family member, don't hesitate to say, "Hey, how about waiting a couple months before you buy that Jaguar or book that cruise to Tahiti or spend a weekend at the casino? What's the rush?" By that time, the bereaved might have regained her financial focus.

Gillikin added, "When a person is grieving, she's vulnerable. If she has received an inheritance, that vulnerability takes on a whole new dimension. Unscrupulous people come in all shapes and sizes and relationships. They'll get closer to the grieving person by encouraging her to talk about her sorrow. Next thing you know, the bereaved has given the other person money. Not because she wants to; it's now simply too hard to say no."

Here, too, when the bereaved is your friend or family member, be watchful. Forget subtlety. Ask her straight out, "Are you being pressured to give someone money?" If she has an existing professional relationship with a lawyer, accountant, or broker, suggest that she make an appointment just to talk. The professional will know what to ask. Look up the phone numbers for her. If she doesn't have any of those professional relationships, encourage her to talk with someone at her local bank.

Professional help in the early stages can help establish long-term financial security.

If you have doubts about her financial stability, ask whether she needs help. Can you and other friends and family members join forces to give or lend her cash? If not, talk with her about items she might sell. Check out what people are buying, and for how much, on Internet sites such as eBay (www.ebay.com). Many towns now have at least one eBay entrepreneur who will sell and ship the items for you in exchange for a percentage. Here, too, advice from her local banker can help protect what little she might have.

One more thing. If your friend doesn't already use a calendar or appointment book of some sort, get one for her. The old-fashioned paper variety is fine. In fact, it might help to flip the pages and see the appointment details written down. Be proactive. Jot down which bills need to be paid on which days. Map it out for at least three months. Financial stability and organization go hand in hand.

81.
Help go through the deceased's clothing and belongings

Letting go of the loved one's clothes and belongings after letting go of the loved one is a daunting challenge. Although many families will go through the clothes and belongings of the deceased together, sometimes there is no family, or family members live too far away to help with this task.

Because the clothes and belongings carry the memories and scents of the one who has died, going through them and deciding what to keep, what to donate, and what to throw away can be not just emotionally painful but exhausting as well. Some people will just close off the room of the deceased for months or years at a time to avoid having to pick up John's favorite fishing shirt or Mother's worn chenille bathrobe.

Also, having lost the loved one, making a decision about which possessions to give or throw away can feel impossible and be immobilizing. The temptation to hang on to everything in an effort to hang on, in some way, to the loved one, is very strong. If you have watched any television programs like *Clean House* or *Mission: Organization*, then you know that people will hold on to things for years and years without ever using or looking at them, simply because they were Mom's or Grandpa's.

You can help avoid this by suggesting that the bereaved call you when he is ready for you to come over to go through those clothes and belongings with him. Offer to bring what is necessary to pack up everything: clear plastic bags or cardboard boxes for donation, plastic see-through bins and labels for storage (for the things they want to keep), and garbage bags for the throw-aways. Also bring packing tape, markers, scissors, and twist ties.

Be prepared to make several trips to complete the job as each item can bring back a memory to savor or cry over. Patience is key to this process. On the other hand, it may go quickly, if the bereaved wants just to get the pain over and done with as soon as possible. It also depends on how much stuff has accumulated over the deceased's life and how family members want to deal with it.

When her mother died, Paula and her sisters, sister-in-law, and aunt gathered in her mother and father's bedroom to go through her mother's closet the day after the funeral while everyone was still there. Laughing at the outdated polyester pantsuits or wrapping themselves in the scent of her, they went through her mother's clothes, each taking items to wear and remember her mother by. It was a communal time of grieving and remembering, and it went quickly.

The rest of Paula's mother's belongings, however, like antiques, cookbooks, and artwork, went slowly and in stages, as her father was ready to let go, as he remarried and remodeled the family home, and finally as he gave away the remaining things to Paula and her siblings twenty-two years later, when he sold the family home.

Like grief, this process has its own time line. Offer to help with it, and be patient.

82.
Keep an eye on her health and safety—and the kids' too

Is your friend getting out of bed each morning, getting dressed,

and doing what activities must be done for general survival—
paying the mortgage, paying bills, grocery shopping?

Is your friend eating? Fix her a meal or take her out for one.
Make individual meal portions in throwaway containers, and
leave them in her freezer with heating or cooking instructions.
Small or light meals are often all that can be managed in the
early stages of bereavement. How's her beverage intake? Liq-
uids are crucial for health; encourage nonalcoholic beverages
because, as mentioned before, alcohol is a depressant.

Is she taking her regular medications? Does she need you to
pick up her medications at the pharmacy or mail order them?
Make a checklist for her to mark when she takes them because
forgetfulness often comes with bereavement.

If your friend is seeing a doctor, offer to accompany her to
record the doctor's instructions. Again, it's too hard for the bereaved, especially if still in shock from a loss, to remember the
doctor's instructions and information.

Is she unable to sleep? Get her a CD with nature sounds
and soothing music. Orange scents sometimes relax people—
but *don't* bring a candle (in case she actually drops off with it
still lit). Or offer to listen or talk in the middle of the night.
Watch for her online, and phone her if she responds to your
instant message.

Equally important if your friend has children is to find out
whether your friend is preparing meals for them. Help her
with that chore. Meals don't have to be fancy, just nutritious.

Peanut butter (ask about allergies) and apples are fine in the short term.

In the immediate aftermath of a death, a responsible adult or two must always know where the children are and what they are doing. Be this adult yourself, and find someone else to help, too. The immediate family is frequently in too much shock to be more than vaguely aware of the children's activities, and the children may stray into danger—or court it for attention.

Is your friend too shaken to drive safely? Drive her and her children wherever they need. Is she locking the doors and windows? Remind her of safety issues and check up on her when you can. That way you'll rest easier knowing she—and the kids—are resting safely.

83.
Be *very* pushy!

Close friends and family can get away with things that neighbors and others can't. This tip requires a little more guts and a closer relationship than Tips #60 and #61, because it is more than just doing a little shopping for the bereaved or inviting him on a ride-along to run errands. Here you use your intimate knowledge of the bereaved to know when it is time to help push him back out in to the world, and when you risk his anger in doing it.

A friend of mine knew this. She called me about a month

after my son had died and told me she was coming to pick me up to go to the apple festival in a nearby town.

"Oh, no, thank you," I said. "I'd rather just stay home."

"You get ready now," she said, "because I'll be there in fifteen minutes."

"No, really, I'm not even dressed. I just want to stay home," I said.

"Well, hop in the shower, and wear something comfortable," she said. "And comfortable shoes. We'll be walking a lot. I'll be there in fifteen minutes."

"I'm not going," I said through clenched teeth. "I'm staying home."

"Fifteen minutes!" she said gaily, as though she didn't know I was angry. "See you then!" she said, and she hung up. I fumed. I cried. I told her off several times, yelling at the ceiling.

Fifteen minutes later, when she arrived, I was showered and dressed. And for one glorious afternoon I felt normal. She walked me to my door and came inside with me to make sure I was settled. I thanked her.

I don't know why my friend's method worked on me that particular day, but it did. Some people have an instinct for when to be very pushy for a good cause. If that describes you, then take it upon yourself to be *very* pushy, find something fun and wonderful to do, and call your bereaved friend to say you'll be there in fifteen minutes. It did a world of good for me!

When you push, use the cues of tone of voice and body language (Tip #31) to determine your friend's state of mind, and remember to be patient but steadfast. Like my friend, don't engage in a debate or argument. Remember, this is about pushing your friend out into the world to distract and help her. Don't shove. Just push. There is a difference.

84.

Remember your favorite fun thing, and do it again!

Whether it is a hike along the beach, a white-knuckle horror movie, or a picnic at the park with the kids, what was fun for the two of you before can be fun again. Returning to places and activities that are anchors for more positive emotions and memories will help the healing process, and might even evoke a surprising smile or laugh, temporarily lifting the cloud of grief.

85.

Buy a subtle gift

Get a special frame for a favorite picture of the loved one. Grief seems to bring out the poet in all of us. A book of inspirational poetry with a focus on grief is a good gift. I enjoyed the ones I received. If his favorite author has a new title out, buy it. Again, reading and enjoying a book by his favorite author is another reminder that not everything from his old life is lost.

There are websites that can help you find appropriate gifts that range from not-too-gushy cards to memorial items for the grieving. Check out the Web resources at the end of this book to find them. Gifts that offer something for the bereaved to do might help. Restaurant gift certificates, tickets to a movie or play, ski-slope passes, free bowling, nine holes of golf, or tickets to a fair, museum, or gallery opening are gifts that prompt the bereaved to get out, move around, and do something different. And it won't hurt that you get to go, too!

Don't be surprised or hurt when your gift isn't used, read, made, or even moved from where he left it when you gave it to him. Just keep trying.

86.
Buy an unsubtle gift

Books on the grieving process might prove helpful to bereaved friends or relatives who just can't talk about their experiences. If the bereaved has trouble communicating her feelings, she may never find out how normal those feelings are. Anger (at the loved one for dying), relief, and feeling abandoned, are all normal responses to a loss. If you've tried repeatedly to discuss these topics and have gotten nowhere, a book could bridge the gap that you can't. There are many excellent books on the grieving process. The bibliography at the end of this book lists some of them.

There are also books on specific types of losses: the loss of a spouse, child, or parent, or the loss to illness, accident, murder, or suicide. These are listed in the bibliography as well.

87.
Remember, it's not only the person who's gone

In her book *Life after Grief*, author Darrelyn Gunzburg reminds us that reactions to the emotional and physical isolation brought about by grief can bring "the unending need to replace the dead with another baby/husband/wife/mother/father, and so on. What someone in grief needs replaced is not the person who has died, but some of the things that person may have contributed to the relationship had they lived, such as love, friendship, physical touch, emotional support, listening, and acceptance."

That doesn't mean the any-warm-body theory applies. Don't say to the bereaved: "You won't have any problem finding someone," or "You're still young. You can have another baby." Instead, be aware that the bereaved might have lost that special someone who winds the clock every Sunday or who makes all the social arrangements; the person who plays the other half of a piano duet or the person who researches vacation options; the spouse who makes sure the oil in the car is changed regularly or the person who always fixes the leaking faucets; the chief cook who had dinner and a hug waiting when he walked in the door every evening; the only friend who really understood his obsession with British sports cars; or the brother who thought he was Superman incarnate.

I'm not suggesting you jump in and fill those roles. I'm just pointing out that, for the bereaved, the fabric of life has been ripped; it's full of holes.

What can you do? Notice the holes. Encourage the bereaved to talk about them. Whatever you do, don't dismiss any of them as trivial. In time, and depending on your own skill set, you can show the bereaved how to fix a faucet or bake a cake.

Losing someone close to us also means losing part of the definition of who we are. When my son died, I lost the person who reflected back to me my definition of myself as mother. When Paula's mother died, she says she lost her primary cheerleader and the one who knew many of the stories of her as a child and a teenager. She lost the person who saw her in the way only her mother could.

Although you can't replace the unique perspective of the deceased, you can ask the bereaved what was unique about their relationship or ask for stories—and then offer to shovel snow from the sidewalk.

88.
Buy her a journal

Most people are not regular journal keepers, so be prepared to jump-start the healing process. And a healing process it is. Studies have shown that, following trauma, journal entries can be highly therapeutic. What's more, they seem to work best when the writer records both the objective details of what happened *and* the emotional information about how things feel or felt.

To help the bereaved get off to a fast start, suggest the ten-ten-ten approach: ten entries, ten minutes apiece, on ten different days. Include a list of ten writing prompts, one for each day, or write one at the top of each of the first ten pages of the journal. Here are some you might consider:

- The best meal we ever shared was…
- His (or her) favorite word was…
- Our favorite holiday was…
- The thing that irked him (or her) more than anything else was…
- If he or she could have lived anywhere, it would have been…
- What I will miss the most is…
- He (or she) was always so proud of…
- When I think of him (or her), one thing I will always remember is…
- One of the most special days of our time together was…
- Looking back and reading again what I wrote these past nine days, what I can see is that…

  In a few weeks, check back to see if the bereaved had a chance to start the journal, and if she would like to share any insights or memories from it.

Don't be critical or pushy if the journal is still empty. The right time will come, and if it doesn't, journaling may not be the right tool for this person. You can always try another approach, such as using one of the prompts to start a conversation. Some people are more comfortable with the spoken rather than the written word. Honor that.

89.
Keep a journal for him

Consider collecting stories and pictures from family and friends and assembling them in a journal as a gift to the bereaved. You can always include blank pages between entries for the bereaved to record his own memories if he wishes.

Be sure to add your own memories as well. Another option is to arrange some specific times, perhaps over lunch, to engage the bereaved in conversation about his memories and feelings.

Consider using a small tape recorder or notebook, with his permission of course, to keep track of these conversations. Write them up on special paper—rice paper or homemade paper would be lovely—and paste them into a journal or ring binder.

90.
Arrange to go to a conference on grieving

When Paula's mother died, her mother's older sister arranged for Paula and herself to attend a workshop on death and grieving at a retreat center near her home. Paula's aunt paid for the airfare and workshop fee so Paula could attend the conference with her. Together, in the mountains of northern California, they learned about the grief process and the steps to take to heal from grief.

Removed from the demands of her young family, Paula had a chance to grieve, to grieve with her aunt, to get some much needed rest, and to eat healthy food. The other benefit for Paula was the stronger bond that developed as she and her aunt shared their grieving for mother and sister. Even today that bond remains stronger and closer than ever.

Check for local programs at religious centers, hospitals, and hospices. They often schedule regular programs on grieving. Don't register just your bereaved friend. Register both of you. Pick her up and drive her to workshop or seminar.

If your budget allows, check with retreat centers and national grief support organizations for conferences and events across the country. Sometimes getting away from the home environment and daily demands gives the bereaved friend a chance to reclaim emotional resources, to gain a new perspective, and to take the first steps toward healing.

As you support her, you also learn something new and deepen the bond between the two of you.

91.
Suggest a support group

A support group can be as simple as three or four people meeting in a park or a quiet corner of a local restaurant to talk about how each one is coping after the loss. Such coping might include sharing memories or getting another's perspective on plans for the future. The camaraderie itself can provide the encouragement to carry on.

Support groups can also be more structured. Most hospitals offer them. At Hartford Hospital (www.harthosp.org), there is a group for spouses aged thirty-five to fifty and another for spouses who are over age fifty. There are groups for families of victims of sudden death or suicide, and for those who have lost infants. There is a group for families whose deceased have become organ donors. Common to all are a comprehensive resource packet, access to material on the hospital's website, short-term grief counseling by phone or office visit, educational programs on grief, follow-up correspondence at designated intervals, and an annual memorial service.

Start by gathering the information for the bereaved. But don't just hand it to him and expect him to take the initiative. Bring him to the meeting. If you're allowed to attend, do so. If you aren't, wait for him. On the way home, encourage him to talk about the experience. He might not be able to articulate why it felt good to be with others of like mind. So don't ask him to evaluate the group's effectiveness yet. Give him time. Take him to the next meeting. Just don't be surprised if, at some point, he wants to go without you.

A friend told me about the astrologer Caroline Casey. In her book *Making the Gods Work for You*, she writes, "We are often intimidated when we encounter people who have undergone breathtaking tragedy. This arises partly out of superstitious fear of tragic contagion…Once we have been to the Underworld [a place of loss and death], the pain of others no longer separates us from them. Fear is transformed into a feeling of poignancy, which is the heart's recognition of kinship. We have earned the right to enter the sphere of another's grief. 'Hi, I see that your passport is also stamped with a visa to the Underworld.'"

92.
Suggest a grief counselor

A grief counselor can help the bereaved make sense of what she is feeling, prepare her for what to expect, and help her reconcile the painful truth that grief is a long process. The bereaved has a right to talk about her loss and relive memories. Not everyone wants to listen. The bereaved has a right to embrace her spirituality and make use of ritual. Some might find that foolish or inappropriate. The bereaved has a right to emotional outbursts. Let's face it; some will find that frightening. As the bereaved travels this long, lonely road, there will come a time when she searches for meaning—the deep kind that provides her with the motivation to do more than just get up each day.

Sometimes, no matter how much you want to help, the bereaved is in a state of despair that requires the assistance of a professional. Don't hesitate to help her find that professional! Check with your state office of mental health. They'll direct you to a host of resources in your area. Do the legwork for the bereaved. Gather phone numbers and websites. You can also contact the American Institute of Health Care Professionals. In fact, a simple search on the Internet will yield more resources than you probably knew existed. Check out some of the websites provided in the Web resources section at the back of this book.

As I've mentioned before, the key here is for you to observe the bereaved, suggest a grief counselor, get the contact information, follow up to see whether the bereaved made the appointment, and then go with her.

93.
Agree with the bereaved

Grief can create an emotional roller coaster, especially if the relationship between the bereaved and the deceased was problematic. In one moment, the bereaved might talk about how kind and loving the deceased was. Next thing you know, the bereaved has nothing good to say about the deceased. Anger can fertilize the litany of faults just as denial can make them disappear. What's a friend to do?

Agree with the bereaved. This is not the time for you to say, "Now, now, he wasn't a total loser. He was always good to the dog," or "Yes, yes, we all know she was a lush. But you must admit she made people laugh." The reverse situation is just as important. With a lump in the throat, the bereaved might say, "Oh, he was the best husband in the world," or "She was the wife of my dreams." In your opinion, he might have been a louse; she might have been a nightmare. There will be plenty of time later for the bereaved to clarify, confirm, or change his feelings about the deceased. What the bereaved wants right now is to have his emotions validated, not challenged.

How do you validate emotions when you don't agree with them? Especially when you're certain that any day now the bereaved's views will turn 180 degrees? Especially when you have good hard evidence to prove your point? You keep your evidence to yourself and say simply, "I know. It must be hard for you." Repeat that. "I know. It must be hard for you."

What you think doesn't matter. Not right now.

94.
Call, call, call

As I mentioned in Tip #69, when Nathan died, my friend Kathy called me every day, sometimes several times a day. How was I? What was I doing? What had I eaten for breakfast? Was today trash pickup day? Did I have library books to return? Did I want to go grocery shopping? What had I eaten for lunch? Did I need to have the oil in my car changed? What did I think of the lead story in the newspaper? What had I eaten for dinner?

At first, I found the calls annoying and told her so. She didn't stop. Had I seen the new book on quilting? Would I go with her to the movies? How was I sleeping?

I snapped at her, "Leave me alone!" Her response? Had I finished the daily crossword puzzle? Did I know the local grocery store had a new produce manager? She had a coupon for buy-one-get-one-free sandwiches. Would I go with her? Did I know anything about shade plants?

She was clever. In my sadness, I once said, "I thought I saw Nathan in the backyard today." She answered, "In the backyard?"

"Yes. He was wearing his yellow raincoat."

"A yellow raincoat?"

"Yes, he loved to splash in the puddles."

"Splash in the puddles?"

"He loved to do that. When he was three, he once came in soaking wet and dirty and just thrilled with himself for getting all the water out of the puddles in the driveway by jumping in them."

"My gosh, he must have been dirty."

"It took me an hour to get all the mud out of his hair."

I know now that what Kathy did is called reflective technique; she gave me back my words and waited for me to fill the silence that followed. Talking about Nathan this way let me keep him alive, even if only in my heart.

One day, I realized just how many times I looked at the phone, waiting for it to ring. Kathy's calls had become my lifeline. I didn't want to get dressed, much less face the world for a sandwich or a movie. I certainly didn't care about produce or quilts or dipsticks. But, oh, how I treasured being able to talk about my son. Somewhere along the line those phone calls made me realize just how much Kathy cared about me, really cared. Slowly but surely, I reached out to grasp the hand she offered. I've never let go.

It was years later that I learned that Kathy sobbed after every one of those phone calls. I was in pain, and she couldn't help. Or so she thought.

Phone calls, not emails. Phone calls. The sound of your voice can be a powerful tool. Use it.

95.
Make him feel needed

All the tips in this book are about helping the bereaved, so this one might sound a little strange. Ask your friend to help. Yep, ask him to help. You might ask for advice or with moving a piece of furniture or some other small personal task, if he is able. But the most effective way to help him is to ask him for help with a volunteer project that helps others. (That's a lot of *helps* in that sentence, but you get the idea!)

Doing something for others reminds your friend that he still has a place and a role in his family, community, business, and religious organization. Feeling needed pulls us out of ourselves, however briefly, and gets us one step further on the road to healing.

When I was grieving for Nathan, my friend Glenda, who published *New England Writers' Network*, a writing magazine, called me whenever the deadline for the next issue was due. After asking how I was doing and listening to how I was feeling, she reminded me that because I was the fiction editor (an unpaid, volunteer position), she had stories for me to look at and a deadline looming. I would protest, but she reminded me how important what I did was, and how the writers valued my critiques. After I agreed to look at some stories, Glenda would tell a funny story or make a humorous remark to leave me laughing.

So ask your friend to help with the next car wash for the church, to serve as umpire for the next Little League game, or to go hold signs with you at a political rally. The exercise, the socializing, or the work will give him something else to think about besides his loss, something else to do besides mourn. And you will both have the satisfaction of knowing you did something to help someone else.

96.

Don't forget the personal holidays

As mentioned in Tip #64, holidays can be a difficult time for the bereaved, especially the first year. Chances are that co-workers, neighbors, and friends will help the bereaved move back into the celebration of the obvious, more communal holidays like Thanksgiving and Christmas, especially if they read this book.

But along with Thanksgiving, Passover, and Christmas are other holidays that—instead of being a time of joy and celebration, of laughter and happy memories, of family, food, and fun—often bring a lonely journey through a wasteland of painful memories and an uncertain future. Certain personal holidays such as anniversaries, birthdays, Mother's Day, and Father's Day all remind the bereaved of the terrible hole that is left in her life by death. And for most of those who are grieving, these are the worst times to be left alone.

As a close friend or family member, you will know what

dates are most significant. It might be his birthday or maybe a wedding anniversary. This is the ideal time to visit, to invite him over to visit, to call, to take her out to lunch, or to remember her and the special day with a card or gift. If you send a card, be honest about your awareness of your friend's grief. Tell her, "I know this holiday must be hard for you this year. I just wanted to let you know I am thinking of you and that I love you." Wouldn't you feel loved and supported if you were the recipient of a card like that?

I did. I belong to the International Women's Writing Guild, which used to hold their summer conference in August, right around the time of Nathan's death. Teaching at the conference kept me distracted from that anniversary, but other holidays were hard.

One year on Mother's Day, I received a card from one of my students at the guild with a message of concern and sympathy. That was so helpful and so important, because even though Nathan is gone, I am still his mother. And every Mother's Day I am reminded of his loss.

Your bereaved friend is still a husband or wife, even though he or she may be widowed. He or she is still a father or mother, a brother or sister, a son or daughter. Trying to pretend that holidays don't happen or avoiding the mention of the loss is not helpful to the bereaved, especially that year of painful firsts—first birthday, first Thanksgiving, first Christmas.

Honesty is much more appreciated and may be an opportunity

for the sharing of both sadness and the recalling of happier times. So remember the bereaved in the marking and celebration of special holidays.

97.
Remember roles in holiday traditions and family gatherings

It's particularly important to ask how the bereaved wants to treat holidays. Some insist that the traditions be carried out and want someone assigned to the tasks of the deceased. Offer to perform these tasks for this family if you know how or can learn. Or help the person assigned to them.

If the bereaved has always had a specific role, ask him to continue in it. If he chooses not to, find someone else or let the tradition go for the year. Check again the next year. Don't let your friend feel his contributions are no longer wanted or that he is no longer part of the holiday. Encourage him to be part of as much as he believes he can handle.

Some families feel having that particular cranberry sauce recipe made will be a sharp reminder of their loss. Find a new recipe and make it instead.

Does he want help finding new decorations? Or help getting out the traditional ones and decorating? Hop to it! Would he rather be away from home in a different and perhaps new setting for the holiday? Offer to host him in your home, or offer to look for a vacation site to enjoy.

If the death occurs over a holiday, offer to put the decorations away for the bereaved or to help him with this task. Mark boxes carefully. Anne's mother never found some of her favorite decorations after her friends took the liberty of taking them down and storing them for her.

The second year of holidays is sometimes harder than the first because the shock has often worn off and too many people expect the bereaved to be over it. They're not. The empty space remains, and you need to remain alert for ways to ease it.

98.
Take care of yourself

No, that is not a mistake. I do not mean take care of them. I mean, take care of yourself.

If you have ever been flying, you know about the instruction that, in the event of an emergency, you should put your oxygen mask on before you help others put on theirs. The reason for this? Well, if you are gasping and choking from lack of air, how helpful are you going to be to anyone else?

Likewise, how helpful are you going to be to your bereaved friend or family member if you are tired, run down, or stressed? How can you lend a shoulder to cry on, an ear for listening, or a hand for helping with meals or moving if you yourself can barely stand?

For some of us, hard times trigger that Superman or

Superwoman response. We rush in to rescue, to fix, to take care of everyone and everything. It can't be done (see Tip #1)!

So make sure you are getting enough sleep, eating regular and healthy meals, and taking time for your family, your work, and some fun. If you have a hard time doing this for yourself, then make an appointment with your friend for the two of you to have a day at a local spa for some pampering and care, or take off for a quiet day of fishing or hiking together.

Whatever you do, take care of yourself. Remember—your oxygen mask first, then your friend's.

99.
Help with the hard decisions

Reason tells us that the best time to make critical decisions is probably not right after life has dropped you over the edge of Niagara Falls in a barrel. But reason doesn't supplement a suddenly lost income, watching the kids while the bereaved heads back to school, or looking out over the backyard each morning at the pool where a two-year-old drowned. Some decisions can't wait, and for those, you can and should weigh in as a fellow problem solver and safety net of support.

Your role here is not to provide answers (you don't have them and neither does the bereaved). Your job is to pose questions, help locate the data that will aid in making the best decisions, and, in time, offer a hand in making the needed changes.

Housing, Job Search, Child Care

With the death of a loved one, especially the breadwinner of the family, financial and other demands can make the future seem painful and unsure. Suddenly, there are so many decisions to be made, many of them significant.

Selling a house is like brain surgery: it is best left to a professional. Still there are ways, short of improving the housing market, that you can give the process a boost. Here are just four:

1. Repair (or find someone who can repair) deficiencies identified in the home inspection or suggested by the realtor. Broken steps, faucets acting like fountains, or bats in the attic can assume frightening proportions when they stand in the way of a closing or threaten to consume precious resources like time or a limited budget.

2. Offer a place of refuge during times the house or apartment is being shown to prospective buyers or while an open house is going on. Listening to people criticize features the bereaved holds dear is neither necessary nor helpful.

3. Send flowers and a light-jazz CD to the house before a big showing. Suggest all the lights be turned on no matter what. One friend showed her home in Tampa fully lit even in daytime, with fresh flowers in several of the rooms and soft music playing throughout. Her only problem was how to deal with the multiple offers that came in the first afternoon it was on the market.

4. Donate three hours of a cleaning service, to be scheduled at the bereaved's request, to tidy up the place before an open house.

Finding a job will be especially challenging for someone who has been out of the job market for a while and is suddenly thrust back into the mix. A life coach can be of great value. Usually priced for a certain number of individual face-to-face or phone-based counseling sessions a month, life coaches can help a person define goals, develop personal strategies, and choose tactics for making the transition back to work smoother and more satisfying. Your role can be arranging an introduction, opening session, or being the financial support for a defined period—say one to three months.

When your friend or loved one is ready to return to work or her social life, offer to take her shopping. Remember back-to-school clothes? This is the grown-up version. Start small, with one perfect outfit appropriate for the job or for the next club meeting. Since life without the deceased means new roles and essentially a new life, consider arranging a makeover at a local salon.

If your friend is looking for a new job, provide names and introductions to businesses and professional friends who can offer informational interviews. This is a less drastic step than asking friends to provide jobs. It may be a cliché that the longest journey begins with the first step, but the nearest job remains pretty far away unless the first contact is made. Informational interviews offer relatively unpressured opportunities to explore how a job or workplace fits with the individual's goals and skills. They also provide needed practice at interviewing, a skill that might well be critical in the next stages of the process.

Prepare a library in a box filled with five books helpful for those engaged in the job-search process. Consider titles like *What Color Is Your Parachute?* along with books on résumé writing and interviewing. Browse your local bookstore or Internet book source for ones that appeal to you. Chances are that they will appeal to the job seeker as well.

Role-play interviews. Stress that the purpose of the interview is not simply to give the company a chance to see and evaluate the candidate but also for the candidate to ask questions and explore whether the job is the right fit. The interview should be treated as a conversation rather than an interrogation. A well-prepared candidate can guide the interview along that path.

Have tasteful business cards printed. Forget the pansies and tropical animals. Choose simple white or cream cards of heavier stock with the necessary contact information printed in black, brown, or navy blue. If the person has a defined profession like teacher, writer, or human resources manager, you can include that as well.

Social Security, Hired Services
If you have a fax machine, offer to send or receive important paperwork for your friend.

If decisions have been made that cannot be changed, support those decisions even if you'd have made different ones.

Research sources of income and assistance, as the bereaved may not have the necessary focus to persevere.

If there are minor children and the deceased is a parent who paid into Social Security, the children can receive support money from the system. If the spousal pair both received Social Security, the children are entitled to the larger of the two monthly payments. When you call Social Security for information (800-772-1213) or go online (www.socialsecurity.gov), have the bereaved and her Social Security number and birthplace with you so Social Security can provide accurate information for her particular case. She may want you to listen so you can write down what is said.

Is a housekeeper needed? A yard man? A fix-it person? A full-time or part-time babysitter? A nurse? A caregiver? Help find these people and check their references. Offer to assist with their interviews. If they're hired, ask your friend how they are working out. If not well, start again. Hiring and firing can be overwhelming for the bereaved.

When Children Lose a Parent or Guardian

There are going to be times when hard decisions have to be made about how to best provide for and care for children when a parent dies. This is unavoidable. When a parent dies, children grieve doubly—first, for the loss of the parent, and second, for the loss of stability in the home. If only one issue gets addressed, the child will still suffer. You have to pay attention to both. Worse, if the child had unresolved issues with the deceased parent, those issues will continue to loom and grow in the child's mind until they cripple the child emotionally, unless somebody helps. In many cases, the surviving parent deals with his or her own grief and may not realize the depths of the child's grief. You can be that somebody.

Talking with the child and listening to his or her fears and concerns is a good first step. Ask the parent whether it's OK to come visit and spend time with the child. You might offer to babysit and give the grieving parent some time away from home or to take the child on an enjoyable outing to a park, a zoo, or any place where it's OK to just sit and talk. Listen to what the child says to you, and reflect back to her—age appropriately—what you hear in her words. The more comfortable children are expressing their feelings, the better off they'll be in the long run.

When a child is still grieving over a lost parent and the surviving parent establishes a new relationship, it is really important to discuss the new feelings with the child in a non-threatening way. If the child is angry with his parent, you can help here, too. Encourage the child to tell you in his own words what he likes—or doesn't like—about the parent's new partner. Without any analysis or judging, acknowledge the child's unhappiness with the new arrangement, and ask what he feels can be done to improve the situation. Reassure the child that even if the parent has a new person in his or her life, that doesn't mean the parent no longer loves or remembers the deceased parent. Once you understand the sources of the child's unhappiness, you can work with the parent to explore ways to soften the blows of change or to work out ways to compromise so that nobody ends up being a villain in the family.

When Children Are Orphaned

If you thought that dealing with a child who's lost one parent was tough, it's even harder and trickier to deal with a child who has been orphaned. Orphans often confront a sense of being without an anchor or even an identity. It's natural for adults to pity children who have lost both parents and to cluck over them and their situation. No matter what else any concerned adults may feel toward the child's situation, everything must be balanced by optimism. If you are dealing with an orphaned child, you must offer hope that the child can continue to live and thrive despite the loss of his parents. This is a message children need to hear many times as they grow up. If the child relies on you, make every effort to be consistent and honest in every interaction. Many times, orphans feel abandoned and later develop serious trust issues. Don't be the source of those issues if you can help it.

Depending on how the child's parents died (in an accident or at different times), an orphaned child may feel guilty about still being alive. Your job as a caring adult is to help the child understand that he is not responsible for his parents' deaths and that the parents would have stayed with the child if they'd had a choice to do so.

Also, when a child is orphaned, offer to provide assistance in readying the child for her move to a new home with family or guardians. The most important thing to remember is to be as honest as you can about what is happening to the family and how the changes will likely affect everyday life. If the child must move out of the local area, you can help by offering to come visit (but keep your promise if you do!) once she is unpacked, and let the child share the new surroundings with you. Help the child to make lists of things she likes—and doesn't like—to share with the people in the new home. This will also help the new caregivers understand what's going on in the child's life and how to best adapt to the new arrangements.

100.
Don't assume the spouse will be able to help

Over the years, long-married couples often wind up looking like each other, but that doesn't mean they grieve the same way. If the bereaved has a spouse or significant other, it's easy for friends and other family to assume that he or she will be emotionally available and supportive to the bereaved.

But depending on who died, the significant other might also be grieving. Or the loss might magnify the significant other's inability or unwillingness to connect on a deep, emotional level. The loss might bring up other issues in the relationship. Both the bereaved and the significant other might feel overwhelmed, ineffective, afraid, angry, and guilty. And because many couples are good at hiding their emotions, you might never know how unsupported the bereaved really is.

How can you help? Follow the other tips in this book. If the bereaved is also receiving emotional support from the significant other, that's great. Just remember, that might not be the case, and any additional support will still be appreciated.

101.
One more time—shut up and listen!

Then listen some more. Remember the definition of death from the first chapter? Death sucks, right? Well, listening to someone talk about death sucks, too. There aren't too many people who want to hear the bereaved talk about her loss. I learned early on that if anyone asked me if I had children, to answer with a simple no. Early on in the grief process, I'd tell people who asked me that I'd had one son but he'd died of cancer. Well, the people I told that to couldn't get away from me fast enough. Very quickly they had an excuse ready to beat it across the room and escape. I don't blame them. Death sucks. But as the bereaved's best friend or family member, you can take up the slack here. (I told you you'd have the hardest job in all this!)

Truly listening is an art. We don't get enough practice at it to perfect our technique. We're used to conversational listening. The kind of listening where we only half-listen while the other half of us composes what we'll add to the conversation when the other person stops talking.

Keep in mind something else from the first chapter of this book. Tip #1: you can't fix it, so don't try. Because you can't fix it, you don't have to come up with your end of the conversation while you listen to the bereaved. There's absolutely nothing you can say that will take away the pain.

The bereaved has almost a physical need to talk about what happened to her loved one, to share memories, to rehash the wake and the funeral. Each telling softens the blow. With each telling, the bereaved heals a little more. Loss is not something you get over, survive, or recover from. There will always be pain from the loss, but it gets easier to bear; the bereaved gets more used to the pain if she can talk about the loss. That's where you'll develop your skills as a true listener. This isn't a two-way conversation you're having. It's a monologue with you as the straight man. You do get to say a few things, but they should serve to keep the bereaved talking: "Oh, yeah I remember that!" "Uncle Bob did look a little tipsy at the wake now that I think about it," "I never knew that about…" or "How did that make you feel?"

Kathy's phone calls to me after Nathan died were a lifeline because she listened and responded just enough to make me feel heard and to keep me talking. So, if that's what you have to do to truly listen, then do it. And the next time you're there for the bereaved, truly listen again.

APPENDIX

ATTENDING FUNERAL AND MEMORIAL SERVICES

OK, so you know there's going to be a funeral or memorial service, and you're worried about going. Your anxiety kicks into overdrive as you fret about how you will follow what's going on if it's all happening in a language you don't speak, wonder what you'll be expected to do or say during the service, attempt to figure out how to avoid inadvertently offending anyone, or even wonder what in the world you should wear. Relax. You're not the first person who's been worried about these things, and fortunately for you, there are plenty of ways to get all the necessary information about funeral customs of faiths and cultures that aren't necessarily your own. Regardless of where the service is held, you'll want to know how to best conduct yourself if you're going to be there. It's a difficult enough time for the bereaved, without him having to worry about educating you in his religious or cultural traditions regarding death while he's burying or cremating his loved one's body.

First of all, not every funeral or memorial service is going to be associated with a religion. While it is true that services are most often associated with religious beliefs, some may be entirely nonreligious in nature. Depending on the circumstances, the service might be held in a funeral home, a church, a temple, a private residence, a crematorium, a public park, a beach, or in a grove of trees. There may be other things that make a service more meaningful to friends and family, too, so it's not going to help you to seek out a "one size fits all" description of Christian, Jewish, Muslim, Buddhist, or Neo-Pagan funerals.

One thing common to every funeral service is this: the funeral, ritual, memorial, or whatever it is called, will be significant in helping the bereaved start her personal healing process. Maybe she'll tear her clothes or wail and moan to show her grief. Maybe she'll sit or stand quietly and receive family and friends in an orderly line. Regardless, it is the bereaved who suffers, and the purpose of the customs and traditions is to give her a way to express her grief and her desires for the spirit and soul of her loved one.

The bottom line, though, is that you shouldn't let the fact that the deceased was a member of a religion or cultural tradition you don't know much about keep you from attending. Here are suggestions for where to find information and help in preparing yourself to go to the funeral or memorial.

If the funeral or memorial service is going to be held at a funeral home, it's always a good idea to call the funeral director ahead of time to get information. The funeral director assists the bereaved in planning and fulfilling religious and traditional requirements, and will also accommodate special requests from the family members. The funeral director will be able to tell you what kind of plans are in place for the service, offer suggestions for appropriate attire, and also tell you whether the bereaved family would appreciate flowers or prefer a donation in the deceased's name to a favorite charitable organization. Funeral directors also sometimes have pamphlets and brochures they can give you that are very helpful in outlining various services.

What follows are some practical suggestions for whom to contact or where to look for information about the most common funeral practices in the United States.

Christian

Clergy are usually available for brief conversations about what to expect, and there is a wealth of information on this topic on both the Internet and in your public library. A phone call to the church secretary will yield valuable information, and church officials will be happy to answer your questions. So do your homework before you go to a Christian funeral—read, call, and ask around.

Cultural differences may play a role in funeral services. Those differences may include the choice of music, whether or not or even how photos of the deceased are displayed on or around the casket, and how comfortable people are with open expressions of sorrow. Protestant funerals usually include hymns, recitations, group prayers, and eulogies by friends and family. Most families ask the church or funeral home to print small programs so that people can easily follow the proceedings during the service. If everyone around you rises, join them.

Geography also plays a role. In many rural communities, getting to the location of the viewing and funeral is difficult, the cost of overnight accommodations prohibitive, and often farmers can't afford to spend too much time away from the farm. In such situations, the viewing and funeral are often held on the same day.

There are no *do* or *don't* colors for your attire at a Christian funeral, though black is predominant. There are no prohibitions against trousers for women or requirements that heads be covered. Funeral attire should be conservative and respectful.

Nonreligious funerals and memorial services

Obviously, if the deceased was not a follower of any religious belief, ceremonies or services for her may take any number of forms. Typically, however, these will be celebrations and testimonials to the value of the person's life, and they will give the family and friends a chance to remember and mourn together. Call ahead to the funeral home and ask the funeral director for information about the service the bereaved has planned.

Nonreligious services may include inspirational readings, recollections of times spent with the deceased, anecdotes and stories, the playing of favorite music, and video testimonials.

A friend of mine went to such a celebration for a doctor who was Jewish but whose wife could be called a secular humanist. About a month after his death, she had a celebration of his life, inviting his family and friends, and even some of the patients whose lives he had affected.

Because they lived out in the country, and he had been an amateur astronomer, at one point she turned off all the lights and invited everyone to look at the stars, which covered the sky like a million lightning bugs. It was a fitting tribute and seemed to help her cope with his loss. Ten years later she still refers to the stars as "his headstone."

Judaic

In all Jewish funerals, a rabbi leads the service. You'll be expected to dress conservatively, and men are expected to wear head coverings. Call the temple to get information about what to expect at the funeral service; even if the rabbi cannot come to the telephone, the temple secretary, the cantor, or any of the community volunteers will be able to address any questions you might have.

Islamic

The Muslim funeral, led by an imam, is a sober event. There won't be any music or singing. Wear modest, dark clothes. To get information about what to expect at the funeral and how to dress appropriately, call a local mosque or contact the Islamic Society of North America (ISNA) at (317) 839-8157.

Buddhist

The Buddhist funeral will be led by a monk or priest. Buddhist funeral services focus on acknowledging the love that has been shared with the deceased. There are no hard-and-fast rules governing Buddhist funerals. They happen in the home, they happen outdoors, and they happen in funeral homes, and the bottom line is that moderation and common sense are what prevails. The funeral itself is almost always simple and dignified.

Dress comfortably, and don't wear anything flashy or showy. In some traditions, it is customary for friends and family to send wreaths of flowers for the funeral, unless there are explicit wishes that charitable donations be made in lieu of flowers. To get information about what to expect at the funeral, call a local Buddhist temple, or ask the funeral director what form the service will take and what appropriate attire will be. While there are also excellent descriptions on the Internet of what form Buddhist funerals can take, much of the Buddhist service is designed around the individual and the family, so these sources may not always correspond to the event you will attend.

Hinduism

Like many other traditions, Hindus believe that no time should be wasted in releasing the soul to continue on its journey. Because Hindus believe the burning away of the body releases the soul to the heavens and the gods, the funeral service will probably happen within one to two days of the death and include cremation. While many funeral homes that cater to Hindus have special cremation setups, some do not, so the service may take place in a facility designed for this purpose.

You can find a lot of useful information online just by entering a search for "Hindu temples USA." Again, it's a good idea to contact the funeral director for specifics about what to expect and how to dress.

Unitarian Universalism (UU)

Each funeral is designed to meet the spiritual needs of the family, and the officiating UU minister and members of the family work together to create something that will be meaningful and comforting to those who attend. Call the UU minister's office, and he or she will be able to help you understand what to expect.

Small, simple floral arrangements, fruit baskets, and donations to the deceased's favorite charities in his or her name are welcome and appropriate. Dress at these services can be anything, but should always reflect respect for the deceased and his family.

Neo-Paganism

The person who officiates at a Neo-Pagan funeral will usually be a priestess who is an experienced member of the deceased's group, most commonly known as a circle, or if the group is Wiccan, a coven. If the service is being held in a funeral home or chapel, the funeral director will have information for you about what to expect. If not, you can ask a member of the family for the contact information for the priestess, who will be glad to explain the upcoming service and the significance of the rituals to you.

Dress comfortably, and don't worry about the color of your clothes. Attire for a Neo-Pagan funeral ritual is best determined by the location. The service itself might be held in a garden, in a grove of trees, on the beach, at a funeral home, or, in some cases, a church.

Baha'ism

Because the burial must happen quickly, some families also arrange for a memorial service later, so that people who cannot arrive in time for the funeral can offer their condolences and sympathies. These funeral services tend toward simplicity, so instead of flowers, you might want to consider giving a card or a small offering of fruit to the family.

Since there is no clergy in the Baha'i faith, all the details of the funeral and memorial planning are left to the discretion of the family members and the Baha'i community. Check the Yellow Pages, and call the Baha'i Community Office, or call a family member to get more information about what to expect at the service.

So, to sum it all up, all of these traditions offer a chance to comfort the bereaved, but they are also a chance to learn about different beliefs, which are both great reasons you should attend. Go to the funeral; help the bereaved. If this book helps you do that, it has served its purpose. Blessed be. Om Shanti, Shanti, Shanti hei. Amen. Good job.

BIBLIOGRAPHY

Adler, Margot. *Drawing Down the Moon: Witches, Druids, Goddess-Worshippers, and Other Pagans in America*. New York: Penguin Books, 1979.

Biegert, John E. *When Death Has Touched Your Life*. New York: Pilgrim Press, 1981.

Bramblett, John, *When Good-Bye Is Forever: Learning to Live Again after the Loss of a Child*. New York: Ballantine Books, 1991.

Casey, Caroline W. *Making the Gods Work for You: The Astrological Language of the Psyche*. New York City: Harmony Books, Crown Publishers, 1998.

Colgrove, Melba, Harold H. Bloomfield, and Peter McWilliams. *How to Survive the Loss of a Love*. Los Angeles: Prelude Press, 1991.

Drescher, John M. *In Grief's Lone Hour*. Scottsdale, PA: Herald Press, 1986.

———. *Strength for Suffering*. Scottsdale, PA: Herald Press, 1969.

Finkbeiner, Ann K. *After the Death of a Child: Living with Loss through the Years*. New York: The Free Press, 1996.

Grollman, Earl A., ed. *Concerning Death: A Practical Guide for the Living*. Boston: Beacon Press, 1974.

Gunzburg, Darrelyn. *Life after Grief: An Astrological Guide to Dealing with Loss*. Bournemouth: Wessex Astrologer, 2004.

James, John W., and Frank Cherry. *The Grief Recovery Handbook: A Step-by-Step Program for Moving beyond Loss*. New York: Harper & Row, 1988.

Jensen, Amy Hillyard. *Healing Grief*. Redmond, WA: Medic Publishing, 1980.

Kaplan, Robbie Miller. *How to Say It When You Don't Know What to Say: The Right Words for Difficult Times*. New York: Prentice Hall, 2004.

Kelly, Lynn. *Don't Ask for the Dead Man's Golf Clubs: What to Do and Say (and What Not to) When a Friend Loses a Loved One*. New York: Workman Publishing, 2000.

Keogh, Martin J. *As Much Time as It Takes: A Guide for the Bereaved and Their Family and Friends*. Charlottesville, VA: Hampton Roads Publishing, 2005.

Komp, Diane M. *Hope Springs from Mended Places: Images of Grace in the Shadows of Life*. Grand Rapids: Zondervan Publishing, 1994.

Miller, James E. *How Can I Help? 12 Things to Do When Someone You Know Suffers a Loss/What Will Help Me? 12 Things to Remember When You Have Suffered a Loss*. Fort Wayne, IN: Willowgreen Publishing, 2000.

———. *How Will I Get Through the Holidays?: 12 Ideas for Those Whose Loved One Has Died.* Fort Wayne, IN: Willowgreen Publishing, 1996.

———. *A Pilgrimage through Grief: Healing the Soul's Hurt after Loss.* St. Meinrad, IN: Abbey Press, 1995.

Mitsch, Raymond R., and Lynn Brookside. *Grieving the Loss of Someone You Love: Daily Meditations to Help You through the Grieving Process.* Ann Arbor, MI: Servant Publications, 1993.

Smolin, Ann, and John Guinan. *Healing After the Suicide of a Loved One.* New York: Fireside, 1993.

Starhawk, M. Macha Nightmare, and The Reclaiming Collective. *The Pagan Book of Living and Dying: Practical Rituals, Prayers, Blessings, and Meditations on Crossing Over.* HarperSanFrancisco, 1997.

Terr, Lenore. *Too Scared to Cry: Psychic Trauma in Childhood.* New York: Basic Books, 1990.

Wolterstorff, Nicholas. *Lament for a Son.* Grand Rapids, MI: William B. Eerdmans Publishing, 1987.

Zunin, Leonard M., and Hilary Stanton Zunin. *The Art of Condolence: What to Write, What to Say, What to Do at a Time of Loss.* New York: Harper Perennial, 1991.

WEB RESOURCES

Grief Organizations

www.adec.org The Association for Death Education and Counseling Professionals (ADEC) is one of the oldest interdisciplinary organizations in the field of dying, death, and bereavement, and the publisher of the *Forum* newsletter. Its nearly two thousand members include a wide array of mental and medical health personnel, educators, clergy, funeral directors, and volunteers. Educational opportunities include the association's annual conference, courses, and workshops, and its certification program.

www.adherents.com Adherents.com has a collection of more than forty thousand adherent statistics and religious geography citations.

www.bereavedparentsusa.org Bereaved Parents of the USA is a national nonprofit organization that supports the newly bereaved, especially parents, grandparents, and siblings. The group offers a national newsletter and an annual gathering, as well as local chapters in about twenty-eight states.

www.centerforloss.com The Center for Loss provides publications and workshops to help grieving people as they mourn transitions and losses that transform their lives. The center helps both mourners, by walking with them in their unique life journeys, and professional caregivers and laypeople, by serving as an educational resource and professional forum.

www.centeringcorp.com The Centering Corporation is a nonprofit organization dedicated to providing education and resources for the bereaved, founded in 1977 by Joy and Dr. Marvin Johnson. It provides educational offerings and workshops for caregivers and families, and publishes *Grief Digest* magazine.

www.compassionatefriends.org The mission of the Compassionate Friends, a national nonprofit, is "to assist families toward the positive resolution of grief following the death of a child of any age and to provide information to help others be supportive." It has chapters and offers regional and national conferences, as well as other resources.

www.funeralplanning101.com Funeral Planning 101 is a compendium of valuable information about various funeral traditions for many faiths.

www.goodgriefresources.com Good Grief Resources was founded by Andrea Gambill, whose seventeen-year-old daughter died in 1976. Twenty-eight years of experience in grief support has provided valuable insights into the unique needs of the bereaved and their caregivers, and wide access to many excellent resources. The primary goal of Good Grief Resources is to connect the bereaved and their caregivers with as many bereavement support resources as possible in one efficient, easy-to-use website directory. The organization also offers several different camps for children who are grieving.

www.grief.net The Grief Recovery Institute, an internationally recognized authority on grief recovery, provides programs for the Compassionate Friends, the National SIDS Foundation, the National AIDS Network, the University of California at Irvine, Chapman University, and many others. The website includes a list of more than twenty articles about helping and healing from grief, along with a list of certification programs to help others in the community, the workplace, and elsewhere.

www.griefjourney.com The Centre for the Grief Journey was established in 1992 to assist and support people through the grief journey and to provide meaningful resources and help. The centre's approach combines education, empathy, and encouragement as part of a comprehensive package of methods and materials. Because there is so little understanding of grief and loss in our death-denying culture, people often fear that they are losing it or going crazy. Understanding that grief is a natural, albeit difficult, experience can free people to explore their reactions and feelings by giving them permission to grieve.

www.griefnet.org The Internet community GriefNet.org is for people dealing with death, loss, and grief, and involves fifty email support groups and two websites. The clinical psychologist and traumatologist Cendra Lynn directs the community.

www.inlieuofflowers.info/index.php?s=14&p=1 This article, titled "Religious Funeral Ceremonies," describes the funeral services of many different religions.

www.isna.net The Islamic Society of North America is dedicated to improving the quality of life for Muslims in North America.

www.shamash.org Shamash: The Jewish Network provides an array of information and discussions, along with links to Jewish community centers and temples.

www.twinlesstwins.org Twinless Twins Support Group International was created to provide a safe and compassionate community along with healing and understanding for the unique grief experienced by twinless twins and other multiples when they lose a twin to death or estrangement.

www.webhealing.com Since 1995, webhealing.com, the Internet's first interactive grief website, has served the bereaved by offering grief discussion boards, articles and links on grief, as well as a memorial page. Tom Golden, who created the site, is an internationally known psychotherapist, author, and speaker on the topic of healing from loss.

Funeral Customs and Information

Leave Donation Programs

Campbell, Bill. "Experiment Proves Successful: Donating Vacation Days to Colleagues Becomes Permanent," Penn State University, www.psu.edu/ur/archives/intercom_1999/Jan28/vacation.html.

"Employee to Employee Leave Donation Program," Maryland Department of Natural Resources, www.dnr.state.md.us/insidednr/humanresources/leave_donation.asp.

"Leave Sharing Programs," Defense Finance and Accounting Service, http://dfas.dtic.mil/civilianpay/leave/leavesharing programs.html.

"Money File: The Vacation Time Donation Program," PBS, www.pbs.org/nbr/site/onair/transcripts/050921_moneyfile.

Establishing Education and Trust Funds
www.savingforcollege.com This website offers information and further resources on financial aid and different funding sources for college.

Grief in the Workplace
www.journeyofhearts.org Journey of Hearts combines elements of medicine, psychiatry, poetry, prose, and images to provide resources and support to those who have experienced loss, be it acute or long standing. This site was designed for those who are in the early stages of grief, loss, and bereavement to provide words of solace, condolence, hope, and inspiration. This site is also for those who are ready to start healing after a significant loss, accept, assimilate, and recover from the loss, and recognize that they are forever transformed. In addition to a two-part article on grief in the workplace, there are also articles and resources on other aspects of grieving and loss.

Video Memorials

www.kdsproductions.com KDS Productions is owned and operated by Adam Dusenberry and Marsha Browne, award-winning, professional videographers with a long history between them of documentary, live event coverage, memoir, and oral storytelling. Between them, they have more than twenty years of experience in broadcast television production and videography. They have received many awards and honors for their productions in national competitions.

Other Resources

www.compassionbooks.com A resource with an extensive selection of books, videos, and CDs, reviewed by trained professionals, to help young people and adults through serious illness, death, loss, and grief.

www.thecomfortcompany.net The Comfort Company sells unique sympathy gifts for someone who has experienced the loss of a loved one, a collection of sympathy poems and cards, and bereavement and condolence gift ideas with the hope of bringing comfort and remembrance to those who are grieving.

ABOUT THE AUTHOR

Liz Aleshire authored *Private Lives of Ministers' Wives* for New Horizon Press; *Bugs: Stingers, Suckers, Sweeties, Swingers* for the First Book Series from Franklin Watts, now a part of Scholastic Books; and the self-published *Willybudkin: A Fireside Tale for Parent and Child.*

As a quilter, she cowrote with her friend Kathy Barach *The Confident Collector's Guide to Antique Quilts* for Crown Publishing, then did a second edition for Random House's Collectibles line, titled *The Official Price Guide to Quilts.* She also wrote hundreds of newspaper and magazine articles. At the time of her death, she was working on a children's book about a young girl, Lily Ann, who was able to travel back in time to meet famous women using the magic of her grandmother's quilt—a story that combined Liz's love of history and quilts.

As well as being an author, Liz was a loved and respected teacher of writing and the writing process, offering her knowledge and experience each year for the past twenty-five years at the International Women's Writing Guild summer conference at Skidmore College in Saratoga Springs, New York; at Manchester Community College in Manchester, Connecticut; and at other writers' conferences and gatherings.

As is the case with many writers, Liz was also a voracious reader who loved to peruse the shelves of used bookstores looking for well-read, well-written books to either add to her collection or give away to her family or her many writer friends.